Choose You!

Reignite Your Passion for Life

by

DR. RACHEL MITCHUM ELAHEE

ISBN: 1502438720
ISBN 13: 9781502438720

TABLE OF CONTENTS

Choose You!

DEDICATION

I dedicate this book to God, who provides constant inspiration. He pours into me and allows me to pour into others.
I dedicate this book to my husband, Darius. Thank you for being my rock, my support, and my love.
I dedicate this book to my four children: Donovan, Christian, Savannah, and Miles. As my husband and I raise them, they teach and mold us, even as we teach and mold them. They unabashedly show me love and don't mind pointing out my faults.

ACKNOWLEDGEMENTS

I want to thank my husband Darius for his unwavering support. He provided space and time for me to write, which is no easy feat with four school-age children. I thank my children for their support and their never-ending questions. They are the first ones that required me to defend why this book is necessary and begged me to let them read it upon its completion.

I want to thank the women who graciously allowed me to interview them and let the world peer into their lives: Pastor Veta Blanding, Jackie Brewton, Jackie Cowan, Dr. LeTosha Gale, Tiffini Gatlin, Stephanie Simmons, Terrilyn Simmons, Jennifer Tacker, Dr. Pamela Thompson, and Judge Allegra Montgomery Walker.

I am deeply indebted to my friend Terrilyn Simmons. In addition to allowing me to interview her for this project, she has been my unofficial media coach, public relations strategist, marketing advisor, and cheerleader, all for the cost of an occasional meal! After strategizing, planning, advising, devising, and writing all day for her paid job, she found time and energy to answer my questions, provide direction, and share her invaluable ideas for me to consider. I also want to thank Dannieka Wiggins who is a fierce editor and public relations assistant. Lastly, I'd like to thank Mickey Parsons, for his unrelenting encouragement through all of my popcorn thoughts and distracting ideas.

ABOUT THIS BOOK

C hoose You! is a book of brief strategies and insights that will resonate with busy, professional women. Reading this book, completing the journal exercises, and applying what you have learned to your life will significantly increase your level of life satisfaction and happiness. Women wear so many hats that a fashion show couldn't keep up with them. It becomes too easy to live reactively, dealing with things as they come. *Choose You!* provides an opportunity for women to slow things down by planning a proactive approach to living. This book of strategies gives women insight into how to approach life by first taking care of themselves. Unfortunately, many women cringe at the thought or feeling of prioritizing their needs and wants over others, in fear that the mere act of doing so is selfish and mean-spirited. What these same women don't realize is that taking care of themselves first is an act of love for themselves and others. It allows them to have more to give to others while staving off life dissatisfaction and stress.

As a psychologist and professional coach, I've had the privilege of working with many women. Although their concerns and needs have varied, too often the common denominator has been their consistent practice of putting the needs of others before their own. Frequently, I say that not only do we not put ourselves on the top of our personal to-do list, most of the time we are not even on the list! Although living life from this perspective is no easy feat, my desire is for women to more frequently choose themselves. I want to hear women report that they looked in the mirror and said to their reflection, "I choose you!" As such, this book serves as a guide for women who continue to struggle with this principle. For those women who do choose themselves but fall off the proverbial wagon sometimes, this book will serve as a gentle reminder.

I wanted to capture very necessary life-coaching strategies in a convenient format. *Choose You!* may be a bedside staple, fit nicely in your purse, or easily downloaded to your favorite e-reader. The strategies in *Choose You!* are short and practical. It is a perfect length for women with busy lives, allowing them to get their brief moment of insight, without having to find that nonexistent free time to read. If you have a few extra minutes, *Choose You!* is a great day-starter, facilitating focus with a side of tea or coffee. It also is a nice accompaniment to an evening of reflection with your feet up and a relaxing glass of vino in hand. Enjoy *Choose You!* any way you choose!

WHAT TO EXPECT

This book of strategies includes quotes, biblical scripture, questions for introspection, anecdotal stories, and journaling prompts, so get a really nice journal and special pen to keep handy as you read.

I have had the privilege to be friends and acquaintances with some amazing women. *Choose You!* includes vignettes from women who have agreed to allow us to peer into their personal journeys to learn more about how they have been able to apply the strategies discussed in this book. Allow me to briefly introduce them to you: *Judge Allegra Montgomery Walker* won a judicial election with all the odds against her. *Coach Jackie Cowan,* a high school girls' basketball coach and math teacher, has won multiple state and division championships and was named Coach of the Year. *Pastor Veta Blanding* is a powerful woman of God who is committed to her family, loves to laugh, and who co-pastors Hopewell North East Missionary Baptist

Church with her husband. *Dr. Pamela Thompson* is a psychologist and author who loves life and loves to learn. *Dr. LeTosha Gale* is a modern physician with old school wisdom. *Tiffini Gatlin* is a former bank manager, mother of three, blogger, and owner of *Tastemaker Magazine. Stephanie Simmons* is a teacher and educational trainer who has a renewed love of life. *Jennifer Tacker* is a dedicated mother and award-winning pharmaceutical sales representative who embraces life with enthusiasm. *Jackie Brewton* is an entrepreneur and gifted motivational speaker who left the corporate world to work with teenagers in academic settings. You will have the opportunity to learn more about these women as you journey through *Choose You!*

ABOUT THE AUTHOR

I am Dr. Rachel Elahee, and I am on a quest to help women live happier, more fulfilled lives. For years, I burned the candle at both ends and in the middle too. I had the business, the kids, the nonprofit—the works. Despite my full plate, I continued to seek new ways to help clients, community, and everyone else who seemed to have a need that fit my skill set. My inability to say "no" and set limits resulted in more chaos. I kept filling my cup until it ran over. The more I gave, the more emotionally depleted I became. I started forgetting things and became less productive. I dreaded hearing the phone ring and opening my e-mail, because I knew more commitments awaited me.

One day, I noticed that I was starting to avoid my life, because at the end of day, I didn't like what it had become. I just didn't want to do it anymore. And that scared me.

So I decided enough was enough. I sat down and took an inventory of my life. Then it clicked. I'd lost my power. I'd lost sight of my goals. I'd lost...me.

I started stripping away everything that didn't add to me. And I replaced that stuff with things that nourished and nurtured my soul—more time with my children, great books, and the clients I knew I could serve best. I found my joy, and creativity came back. Things felt more balanced, vibrant, and alive.

I was reintroduced to the woman I used to be. And I discovered I'd missed her.

During my personal process of awakening, I was inspired to help other women who were on the same journey...women who needed to hit the reset button and refocus...women who needed to reignite their fire.

Let's reassess your goals, rediscover your passions, and reclaim your power. Your career, your family, your spirit—you. It can all coexist. If you'll trust me, I'd like to show you how.

One

YOUR LIFE IS NOT A DEMOCRACY

 $\mathcal{W}$ hen it comes to the opinions of others about your life, majority *does not* rule. Let others' opinions remain their opinions and not the linchpin upon which your life becomes contingent. The only way their opinion counts is if you count it. Acting on what others want for you requires *your implicit or explicit approval.* While we hope that neighbors, friends, family, and strangers have your best interests at heart, they do not have the right to insert their agendas into your life without your approval. Let the last part of that sentence marinate. Galatians 1:10 NIV asks, "Am I now trying to win the approval of human beings, or of God? If I were still trying to please people, I would not be a servant of Christ."

Personal Insight: The votes have been cast. Whose are you counting?

PERSPECTIVES: THE COMPANY YOU KEEP

*C*oach Jackie and Pastor Veta provide their perspectives on how they are impacted by others.

Coach Jackie

Coach Jackie has led her high school girls' basketball team to repeated division wins and several state championships. In March 2014, after her smallest team to date—only seven players—won the state championship, defeating a team with fifteen players, she was named Coach of the Year. Beyond being well respected on the court, Coach Jackie is unilaterally highly esteemed for her vision, confidence, love, and leadership.

Regarding the impact of others, Coach posits, "People only do what you allow them to do. We all have the ability to determine who interacts with us and to what capacity, based on what we're engaged in."

Pastor Veta

Pastor Veta possesses an abiding faith and love for others. With her fun-loving and joyous nature, she has an uncanny ability to make everyone feel special, even if she doesn't know them.

Pastor Veta's sage insight reveals, "There are people who can surround you and impact your life negatively and positively; it just depends on what you allow to filter in."

Two

"NO" IS A COMPLETE SENTENCE

"*N*o" is small but a strong enough sentence to support itself! You do not have to follow it with apologies, excuses, or explanations unless you want to. Saying no does not mean you are mean-spirited or rude. You do not need to provide reasons or justifications for your choices and decisions.

If a straight no seems too harsh or inappropriate, you can use these simple steps:

» Ask for more details if necessary;
» Compliment the other person ("That sounds like a great idea!");
» Give your decision ("No"; "I am sorry, I won't be able to participate"; or "Let me think about that and get back to you"); and
» Close ("Thank you for thinking of me").

When asked to do something, ask yourself these questions:

» Do I want to do it?
» Do I have time to do it?
» If I say yes to this request, am I saying no to something that is a priority for me?

Personal Insight: What is difficult about saying no to people you know? Is it more or less difficult to say no to strangers? If saying no is difficult, why do you think that is the case? How often do you say no to yourself because you have felt compelled to say yes to someone else?

Three

DO NOT TAKE "NO" PERSONALLY

*W*hen others tell you "no", are you easily offended? If so, let me assure you that there is no reason to take offense. Most likely, the response you received is not about you. A no only means no to your request or not right now; it does not mean the person does not like you. "No" does not mean you are not intelligent. It does not mean your idea is ridiculous. It does not mean a lot of things you may be catastrophizing it to mean. Not to sound harsh, but people have considerations, obligations, and concerns other than you. It is commendable that they are taking care of themselves and their priorities. Not only do they have the right to say no, but you have no right to expect them to put their needs before yours. (Sometimes it feels nice when someone does put your needs first, but consider that a bonus, not an expectation.) You can ask the reason for the no or ask if it's okay for you to check in with them again in a certain period of time. Regardless of which choice you make, lighten up. The "no" is not always about you.

> *Personal Insight: Think of a recent time when you made a request of someone and they told you no. How did hearing that make you feel? Rejected? Disrespected? Annoyed? Relieved? Looking back on it now, could there have been some other reason (other than it being a personal statement about you) for the no you were given?*

Four

PRACTICE SAYING YES TO YOURSELF

W hen you say no to the things you do not want to do or are not able to do, you are saying yes to the things that you want to do. You are saying yes to your priorities, values, and goals. You get to say yes to family and friends. You get to say yes to *whatever you want* because *you love you,* and you get to spend your time doing *whatever you want*! (Notice the none-too-subtle emphasis on *you*.)

God gave us twenty-four hours in a day. Since the day is time-limited, you may not be able to accomplish everything you want for yourself as well as everything that everyone else wants and requests of you. Have you ever wondered why we are so quick to say yes? Perfect, because I am here to tell you. We say yes because we want to be liked, we don't want to let people down, we like to be seen as helpful, and we enjoy being thanked. We like acknowledgement—yes, even those of you who like to stay out of the limelight. But saying no to others allows you to say yes to other opportunities that are important to you.

Need another good reason to say no to others and yes to yourself? If you find that your focus, energy, resources, and attention are being drained, chances are good that you are not saying no to others. Say no, so you can say yes. Saying no does not mean that the object of the no is a bad thing; it just means that it is bad *for you* right now. Maybe it's a person, job, or past-time. The solution? You have to draw the line somewhere and limit your activities. If you do not respect your own time, why should others respect it? *You can do it!* (That was my Bobby Boucher/Adam Sandler voice from *The Waterboy*.)

Personal Insight: What are the things you choose to say yes to? What are your priorities? Consider what's important to you spiritually, emotionally, and physically. Put your priorities in your calendar or on your "Must Do" list.

Five

ENCOURAGE YOURSELF ALONG THE WAY

W e wait so long to pat ourselves on the back that by the time we do, our muscles are stiff and inflexible. Actually, I am being generous. Too often, we do not praise ourselves at all! (Shaking my head.) Sometimes we want recognition from others, but we are reluctant give it to ourselves. It is too easy to engage in negative self-talk. We say things like "I am so stupid. I won't be able to finish this. It's too hard!" Instead of trashing ourselves, we should try to use positive self-talk. Tell yourself, "Good job! That was tough, but I am proud of how I got over that hurdle."

A friend of mine recently participated in a triathlon. She talked to herself throughout the competition and found this to be an effective strategy for self-evaluation. At one point, she felt like she was dragging behind and began asking herself, "Why are you swimming so slowly? Are you okay? Are you hurt? What's up with you; can you go faster? Come on, let's go! Pick it up!" As she got on her bike and began to pick up speed, she continued to encourage herself. You need to encourage yourself. You must adopt the mindset that you are the sole participant in a race you are trying to finish well.

> *Personal Insight: Does it feel weird to give yourself encouragement? How can you make it more of a habit? Identify something you recently worked on for which you could have given yourself positive encouragement.*

$\mathcal{S}ix$

YOU DESERVE TO DO SOMETHING
FOR YOURSELF

Too often we take care of others better than we take care of ourselves. We do not think we *deserve* to put ourselves first. I am going to try a Jedi mind trick you won't see coming. Do you think your sister, best friend, or favorite co-worker should make taking care of herself a priority? What makes you different from her? Does she deserve better than you? Okay, maybe you did see it coming. Surely, you see similarities between yourself and the people you just thought of. If they deserve to do something for themselves, so do you. Challenge yourself to spend time focused on you. This tip is easy on the ears but a challenge to complete. It sounds good, but putting it into effect on a regular basis is a formidable task. First, you have to know what you want to do for yourself. Secondly, you have to value what you decide to do for yourself. Lastly, you have to schedule what you have planned to do. For example, I do not get enough quiet time. I decided to make it a priority and scheduled it in the morning, thirty minutes prior to the rest of my family waking. Doing something for yourself does not have to be dramatic and time-consuming. It can be reading, stretching, or even writing in your journal.

> *Personal Insight: Use your imagination and list all the things you would want to do for yourself. Please note that if getting your hair and nails done is already part of your regular routine, do not dare add it here. That is regular maintenance and does not count. Sorry. This is about doing something for yourself that you have put off doing for far too long.*

Seven

GET A FRESH PERSPECTIVE

*E*verything is new and exciting! Even what was old and boring yesterday can be new and interesting today. Every day is a new day; treat it as such. Refresh your thinking. Refresh your energy. Refresh your perspective. Yesterday is gone. Do not face today as though it's a continuation of yesterday. Today has new promises and new possibilities. Even the Bible affirms this sentiment in Lamentations 3:23 NLT: "Great is his faithfulness; his mercies begin afresh each morning."

Personal Insight: Use your imagination to picture all the great things that are possible for today's tasks. Is there anything that will help to elevate your excitement and energy? Music, scripture, a motivational speaker, or a brief word with a high-spirited friend can help shake off a bland attitude.

PERSPECTIVES: PASSION

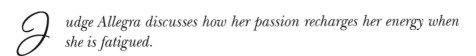

udge Allegra discusses how her passion recharges her energy when she is fatigued.

Judge Allegra resigned from her position as Assistant District Attorney to campaign for the May election that was just over four months away. Most times when Allegra and I talked, she'd already attended three to four engagements that day. She went from meeting to meeting and event to event. She strategized, walked, smiled, listened, explained, and shook hands—most days for most of the day. And this was sandwiched between being a wife and mother in the mornings and evenings. I knew my friend was tired. When I queried as to how she could maintain such a pace, she assured me that she went to bed exhausted every night, but because she was passionate about the positive impact she could make in both the community and judicial system, she woke up every morning excited and ready to campaign. She added, "In addition to my passion, I had a healthy fear of failure. Failure was not an option so I knew I had to do everything I could to be victorious." Judge Allegra's response was a nice *reminder that your body may be tired, but your passion will wake you up and reinvigorate you.*

Eight

GET BACK TO THE BASICS

Have you ever been humming along in life, and your emotional or physical health suddenly began to deteriorate? Maybe getting enough sleep or managing your weight or irritability were not problems initially, but they have become issues over time. When things start to get out of whack, we feel stressed, unmotivated, tired, and physically ill! When you cannot figure out why you feel this way or how you got this way, it is time to *reset*. Start over by implementing the simple basics into your daily routine. For optimal success, do not try to transform everything at once.

Pick one area, and when that is better and you are able to sustain progress, get to work on the next area. Here are some examples of the basics: Eat healthy. Drink water. Get more sleep. See your physician for a checkup. Take walks. Laugh a lot. Have fun. Smile. Pray. Do something interesting or something soothing like cooking, drawing, or gardening.

> *Personal Insight: We make life way too complicated. Take inventory of your life areas that need attention. How would you go back to the basics? How could you simplify? For example, if your diet and digestion is out of whack, a simplification would be to reduce processed food, fast food, sugar, and caffeine. Add in more fruit, vegetables, lean protein, water, and exercise.*

Nine

ARE YOU COMMUNICATING CLEARLY?

*M*y toddler son's no means no, but his no also means yes. Confusing, huh? Sometimes we send out mixed messages to others. We need to be sure that what we say is what we intend. If I mistake my toddler's no for yes, he will holler, "NO, MOMMY, No! No! No!" But remember, as a toddler, he is still learning to communicate. Are you trying to figure out how this applies to you?

Sometimes, when others misinterpret our responses, we get angry and frustrated and respond like my son. But wait, check yourself. What exactly did you communicate? What did you say? Be responsible for the message you send to others. Do not assume it is clear to them just because it is clear to you. Check that they understood your message. Additionally, check that you understand other people's messages to you by responding with statements like "So you are saying…?" or "If I am understanding you correctly…."

> *Personal Insight: Think about recent conversations or directives that you gave that were not executed by others the way you wanted. What could you have done or said differently?*

Ten

ARE YOU SURROUNDED BY DRAMA?

*D*rama happens...in relationships, workplaces, social media, and wherever else there are people. Drama increases stress and reduces productivity. Of course, you know this already because if this title caught your attention, you are likely experiencing drama. To minimize the effect drama has on you, consider the following:

» Identify the source of the drama. Is it several people or one or two?

» Take note of how the drama impacts you—is it a minor or major nuisance?—to determine your next move. If it is a minor distraction, ignore, do not engage, and keep moving. However, if it is a major issue for you, your tactics must change. Talk to the culprits about the impact of their behavior on your work and offer specifics on how they could change their behavior to bring a win-win resolution.

» Identify the steps you can take to distance yourself from the drama. For example, if someone always calls you with foolishness, stop taking their calls or keep the calls very short. Be ready to end the call when the drama discussion begins. If someone always seems to tell your personal and confidential business, limit their access to that information. Do not fraternize with drama starters.

» Address the issue at it is core. For example, "Grace, I like working with you, but I am not interested in gossiping about Olivia. The negativity is really creating a tense and stressful work environment. Maybe you should meet with Olivia directly or the two of you sit down with a supervisor so this can finally be squashed." If you choose this approach, there may be do not be backlash. Nevertheless, continue to be firm. Kudos to you for calling it out and letting the perpetrator know your concern.

» Talk to someone in authority about your concerns, including how the drama is affecting morale and productivity.

Personal Insight: Be specific about the drama around you. Brainstorm your best courses of action.

Eleven

WHAT ARE YOU SAYING BEFORE YOU SPEAK?

*B*efore you open your mouth, assumptions have already been made about you and your credibility. Your resume, social media posts, written communications, social circles and networks, and of course, your nonverbal communications *tell a story*. But do they tell the story you *want* to communicate? If you are striving to thrive professionally, spiritually, or socially, keep this in mind. If I were to look at who you hang out with and who posts on your social pages, what impression will I get? Are your personal and professional connections on social media separate? Just because you love them or like them does not mean their posts should show up in your feed. Think about where you go, what you say, and who you reach. Let your works, words, and whereabouts speak for you. You do not have to be perfect, but know that a blemish in one area could impact the whole picture.

> *Personal Insight: What are the messages you want the world to receive about you? Do these messages line up with your personal and professional goals? Are these goals and messages reflected in both your nonverbal and written communications? Is there someone close to you that you can ask to provide you with an unbiased perspective?*

Twelve

DO YOU HAVE A PERSONAL BOARD OF DIRECTORS?

$\mathcal{A}$ personal board of directors consists of your go-to people. An example of a board member is a close confidant that you trust when you need to talk; other board members may be prayer partners, exercise partners, or mentors. Consider including a person who can help you make important financial decisions, a friend who makes you laugh so hard your stomach hurts, and someone who will lovingly tell you when you are wrong and advise you accordingly. Proverbs 11:14 NKJV says "Where there is no counsel, the people fall; but in the multitude of counselors there is safety." In other words, you are the MVP! You couldn't accomplish this major feat alone. Who are your teammates?

Note: The personal board of directors is not to be confused with the tip in *Your Life Is Not a Democracy*. Your board of directors does not make decisions for you to implement. They provide trusted information for you to consider.

> *Personal Insight: Who is on your board? What need do you have in your life that is not accounted for on your board of directors?*

Thirteen

DO YOU PREFER TO GO IT ALONE?

*H*ave you lost your faith in others? Do you find yourself thinking, "If I want it done right, I'll do it myself"? This has its merits and its drawbacks. Or do you think, "I can do bad all by myself." These core beliefs are baggage that weigh down your spirit. Most likely, these sentiments originate from experiences where you have been hurt in some manner. For the sake of your emotional health, it is imperative that you believe there are good people in the world who will not use and abuse you. It may take some introspection and psychotherapy to help you understand how to avoid picking the wrong people to let into your heart and your life. Please know that being a Lone Ranger with a mistrust of others is not healthy. Genesis 2:18 NKJV reads "It is not good that man should be alone." Similarly, part of English poet John Donne's "Meditation XVII" reads "No man is an island, entire of itself."

> *Personal Insight: What is your core belief about relationships with others? If you prefer to permanently avoid others because of hurt and pain, that's not healthy. The emotional wall and isolation that result not only keep out those who can harm you, they also keep out those who can help you heal. Sometimes healing requires outside influences that are spiritual or therapeutic in nature.*

Fourteen

GET IN POSITION

When children are toddlers, they are too young to be infected and affected by cultural limitations, expectations, self-doubt, and all the other conditions that damper our natural abilities. When young children excitedly anticipate something they want, they run to get into position. When my toddler wants milk, dinner, snacks, or a toy, I tell him where to go to get in position. "Go get in your high chair," or "Go sit on the couch." He is obedient and runs to get in position for what he wants. When there is something I want for him but he doesn't want for himself, getting

34

him to sit still is quite the challenge! As we get older, we can easily be limited by cultural and environmental shoulds and should nots. Instead of being motivated by our desires, too often the disapproval or approval of others becomes our principal motivator. How can this apply to your life?

» Know what you want.
» Be obedient and disciplined.
» Run; do not tarry.
» Get in position.
» Enjoy what is coming your way.

Personal Insight: What do you need to do to get into position?

PERSPECTIVES: YOUR PURPOSE

*C*oach Jackie, Pastor Veta, Jackie Brewton, and Tiffini discuss how they know they have lined up with their life's purpose.

Coach Jackie

"I was approached about coaching when I got out of college, and I responded, 'Oh no, that's not for me.' But it's interesting how God will use people to put you in a position, the place you need to be. So for me, I realized that I had a connection with teenagers.

When I put that connection together with the youth groups in my church, then I could see Him putting me in a position to mentor young teenagers. I could mentor girls through basketball coaching and to take it even further, through some of the things that I've done in Africa. You kind of look back on it and you're like, 'That's what I'm supposed to do.' It's been a combination of events. There is a fulfillment that comes with what I'm doing, as well as ease. Even though it can be stressful and frustrating, it never really feels like it's a job."

Pastor Veta

"When I was called to preach, I hadn't imagined myself as a pastor, maybe the biggest reason being that I didn't see female pastors. It wasn't acceptable in our circle, but then God spoke to me, and I knew. But even in pastoring, you're still evolving. There's something I've always desired to do—and it's going to sound really strange for a pastor to say this but—I've always wanted to do stand-up comedy. Now I get a chance to practice it every Sunday on our congregation. It was easier for me to go into preaching and teaching than it was to stand up there and make people laugh, but every chance I get, I love to see people happy. So that's another piece of my work that creates joy in my life."

Jackie B.

Jackie enjoyed a successful in career corporate America but knew it wasn't fulfilling. She was destined to pour into the lives of others. Jackie has since followed her passion, pouring into middle- and high-school students daily. The letters written by students who attended her classes evoke both joy and sadness and are testimonies of the significance of her work.

"In my corporate career, I was very successful, but I wanted to be significant. Successful people add value to their own lives. I wanted to add value to someone else's life. That was much more rewarding."

Tiffini

As an assistant vice president of consumer and small business banking, Tiffini began to recognize that she had a lot more to offer, and it couldn't be found in her office. She's a wife, a mother of three, and a blogger. Tiffini founded and published Tastemaker Magazine, a digital bimonthly lifestyle magazine for millennials. She successfully manages to stay in the know about Atlanta happenings while staying active in her children's lives.

"I always knew I was destined to be an entrepreneur, I just didn't know in what capacity. I was always the type to climb and look for more…another level…another title. I got to the point where I kept hitting the ceiling. I knew I was reaching my expiration date. Even though the money was good, I had flexibility, and I managed over three hundred people, I was depressed when I pulled up to my job. I recall pulling into my parking spot one day. I was crying, and my stomach was hurting. I was applying for other jobs within the company, and I kept getting turned down. For some of the positions, I was overqualified. Later I realized God was putting up barriers. I wasn't supposed to be there, and He blocked my attempts to stay. I had a college professor who said, 'You will never be content, never be fulfilled until you find your passion.' I found my purpose. I love the work I do now. This is what I am supposed to do, and I know nothing will get in the way. I'm a change agent, and I'm telling the story that isn't being told."

Fifteen

EVERYTHING THAT COMES UP DOES NOT HAVE TO COME OUT

There will be many times when it's prudent to practice self-control. Your feelings may be valid, your observations on point, and input may be necessary. However, it is not always wise for you to speak right then (or at all). But when you do offer your two cents, consider not speaking out of emotion, particularly strong or negative emotion. I once worked with the vice president of a university whom I considered to be very wise, professional, and polished. She told me that when she gets very angry, she writes the offender a letter in which she explicitly expresses herself, telling the person exactly how she feels. After appropriately venting (even if she is still irritated), she destroys the original emotion-filled letter and rewrites it with clarity and professionalism.

> *Personal Insight: Have you ever spoken out of emotion at the wrong time? What were the consequences? What lessons did you learn?*

Sixteen

CRY AND DRY

Sometimes, when my children were hurt as toddlers, they just needed a quick cry and to be comforted. Before I could finish hugging and kissing them, they would wiggle free and be off to the next adventure as their tears dried.

When you fall down, acknowledge the pain. Cry. Vent. And if you are so inclined, even have a *very brief* pity party. Then wiggle free and go at life again, full throttle. Too often, we continue to

43

bemoan our falls and whine about the pain. The fall is over, and the pain is gone. Stop nursing your phantom injury.

> *Personal Insight: When you fall on life's court, do you take your ball and go home? Do you lay there until you are carried off the court? Or do you limp off the court, bandage and ice the injury, and get back in the game? How does the way you handle your injuries help or hinder you?*

Seventeen

REST FOR OPTIMAL PERFORMANCE

*T*oddlers are busy and curious. They play hard. When they tire themselves out, they are not at their best. In fact, they often end up at one of two extremes: grouchy or goofy. To be at their best, sleep is required. When my oldest child was three years old, we couldn't get him to take naps because he just wasn't sleepy. However, we required him to lay down and rest.

Too often, we think it's okay to go, go, go without proper rest. We delude ourselves by thinking we can function optimally with poor rest. Some people even brag about all they accomplished with little or no rest. Rest rejuvenates us physically, spiritually, and emotionally. Researchers indicate that people who get ample rest lose more weight than those who do not get adequate shut-eye. Take care of yourself and stop being hardheaded! Your body requires rest, recuperation, downtime, a break, a power nap. Call it what you will, but do it. Rest is a basic need. If we didn't need it, God wouldn't have gifted us with it.

> *Personal Insight: Are you getting good rest? If not, identify why and what steps you are willing to take to address this issue.*

Eighteen

WHO HAS HELPED YOU ALONG THE WAY?

*A*cknowledge your supporters and take a moment to reach out to them and extend your gratitude. My parents have owned their convenience store for over forty-five years. For many years, it was open twenty-four hours a day, and my father worked third shift. It always makes me proud to hear customers tell my father how he had given them sage advice and encouraged them during really tough times. Often these people would stop for snacks, cigarettes, as well as my dad's counseling in the middle of the night. Who in your life has always been there for you?

Personal Insight: Whose shoulders have you stood on? Take a few minutes to call or write a letter to let them know you appreciate them.

Nineteen

DO YOU COMMUNICATE LIKE A LEADER?

Observe how leaders speak. What do you notice about their tone, posture, eye contact, content, etc., that's different from your own? Take note of the similarities and differences you notice. James Hughes wrote, "Every time you have to speak, you are auditioning for leadership." The ability to listen is another vital leadership trait. William Arthur Ward said, "We must be silent before we can listen. We must listen before we can learn. We must learn before we can prepare. We must prepare before we can serve. We must serve before we can lead."

> *Personal Insight: There's a lot written about leadership. What is your philosophy of leadership? What leadership qualities do you possess? What areas need additional development?*

PERSPECTIVES: LEADERSHIP

*W*e all have the capacity to be leaders. Below, Coach Jackie, Dr. Pam, and Dr. LeTosha share their views on integral leadership traits.

Coach Jackie

"My leadership philosophy is to treat people the way you want to be treated. Be a good follower as you are leading and consider everybody and their situation. Also, it is important to not judge. I think when we begin judging and making unfair assessments of people, then we become weak leaders."

Dr. Pam

When Dr. Pam wants to experience something, learn something, or go somewhere, she makes it happen. She leads a joy- and faith-filled, purposeful life. The significant trials that she has suffered in her life have refocused and matured her. Now, Dr. Pam embraces life to the fullest.

"The best leaders don't ask you to do something they are not willing to do themselves. The best leaders are servant leaders. They operate with a sense of humility. They accept feedback and can laugh at themselves. They recognize the gifts of those they work with and manage productivity plans around those strengths. That is important, because people get burned out if they're not working in their strengths. The best leaders do what they say and say what they mean. Therefore, it'd be unlikely to find a great leader who isn't following their own rules, advice, and procedures; great leaders not only enforce rules and procedures, they work with the team they lead to follow those procedures. Although they make mistakes too, as integral leaders they own their mistakes, and they don't look to blame others. Great leaders embody the essence and definition of leading without boundaries."

Dr. LeTosha

"Really great leaders have servant hearts. They don't lord over the people. Leaders lead among the people. When you lead among the people, you take on the burden with the people. When you do this, the people can see the leader doing the work as well."

Twenty

GETTING OTHERS TO CHANGE

Typically, there is a pattern to our relationships. When you do X, the other person does Y. This holds true for any type of relationship including those that are peer, supervisory, romantic, or familial in nature. Regardless of the situation, I can usually guess how my spouse, children, parents, siblings, and friends will respond when I tell them something. How is this possible? Because we have a long-standing history that includes many conversations over many topics. I can accurately guess their response because of time-tested data. I don't have super powers in this area just because of my psychological background; you can do it too.

Because we are locked into patterns, the way to increase the chances that you will get a different response is for *you* to do something different. Break the cycle of predictability. If the silent standoff between you and your spouse usually lasts for a week, and you want to change that pattern, do something radically different—like not participating in the silent treatment! Do not be discouraged if you do not see behavior change from the other person right away. Be consistent and persistent with your new behavior. If you slip back into your old routine, you are much less likely to see behavior change from the other person. Lastly, be positive and loving in your expectation and desire for change. Realize that you are half of the reason that your relationship is in the state it is in.

Personal Insight: Think of your relationships as a house. Which room needs a makeover? What steps can you take to spruce things up?

Twenty-One

NO WORK, NO REWARD

I have clicked my heels, wiggled my nose, and nodded my head only to discover that the *Wizard of Oz, Bewitched,* and *I Dream of Jeannie* strategies do not work in my life! Sometimes, I have to get really honest with myself and say (or whine or pout), "I don't want to do it." Then I ask myself, "if you don't, who will? If I can't come up with another player, then I am next at bat. I shake off the negative sentiment and adopt the mindset that I want to do it, and I will do it well. There is only one way to get what you want: get busy. Work. Engage. Do. Perform. Pursue. Undertake. Create.

Now, of course I know that you know how to work; you have accomplished some impressive feats. But there comes a time when you get weary and frustrated. Take your rest break. Take a deep breath. Then pull yourself up and get at it. Your reward awaits. Colossians 3:23–24 NLV affirms this: "Whatever work you do, do it with all your heart. Do it for the Lord and not for men. Remember that you will get your reward from the Lord. He will give you what you should receive."

> *Personal Insight: What have you been slacking on? What is the reward that awaits you if you get busy and complete your task?*

Twenty-Two

HOW DO YOU TALK TO YOURSELF?

*Y*our thoughts have a significant impact on your mood and your productivity. Be encouraging, challenging, loving, honest, and optimistic when you talk to yourself. Sometimes to override negative self-talk, you may have to talk to yourself out loud and even answer yourself. (No, it does not mean you are crazy! But you may want to consider who is around…I'm just saying.) We can be more harsh and critical of ourselves than others. Sometimes it's warranted, and sometimes it's just abusive. *Psychology of Women Quarterly* showed that 93 percent of college-age women engage in "fat talk"—conversation in which women criticize their own weight and bodies with their friends. Can you imagine the results if you constantly spoke to yourself with positivity and love?

Personal Insight: Observe your self-talk for a day. What did you notice about the nature of your self-talk?

PERSPECTIVES: PERSONAL VALUE

*D*r. Pam shares her views on one's personal value.

"Your life is evidence of your value. If you feel inadequate, that is an indicator that you need more of something. You have to determine what that something is."

Twenty-Three

CHRONICALLY BUSY

Have you ever witnessed or been a part of a conversation where the topic of discussion was how busy everyone was? Did it appear to be a contest of stress levels and busyness, wherein one story had to be topped by the next? Just as anxious people can make you feel anxious, conversations about overwhelming stress are unfruitful and can increase the stress you already feel. For some, a chaotic existence is a daily, nonstop experience and can easily lead to a stressful and unhealthy existence. Stop rolling your eyes at the book. I know you are feeling exasperated and thinking,

"Sure, Dr. Rae. That's easy for you to say, but you do not understand my life. It's impossible for me to make the changes you're talking about. You don't understand my job and the other issues I face. Furthermore, it's just me. No one else is helping." Well, my response to you is to get an outside perspective on where you can insert help or squeeze in more time for non-stressful activity. You may not have stress-free, perfect days, but if your stress level can come down a notch or two, wouldn't that be progress? Another word of caution…as much as you grumble about wanting to slow your pace and decrease your stress, you will find that difficult. Here are some common problems:

» Issue: You are addicted to the stress.
  Solution: Find a less stressful activity to occupy your time.
» Issue: Your identity has become synonymous with busy.
  Solution: Redefine yourself. What you do is not who you are.
» Issue: You miss the adrenaline rush, and now you are bored or feel useless.

Solution: Replace these activities with something less stressful and more enjoyable, or you will just get busy and stressed again.

Personal Insight: Why are you chronically busy and stressed? What needs to change? What will you eliminate and implement for you to slow your pace? Oh yes, you are responsible for slowing your own pace. Remember, nose wiggling and head nodding only work if you are starring in a 60s sitcom.

Twenty-Four

ESTABLISH TECHNOLOGY-FREE
ZONES AND TIMES

C ell phones, tablets, e-readers, and laptops are great tools for work and fun. However, they aren't appropriate for use in every situation. How present are you for the people who are in front of you if you are always looking down at your phone? And what about the impact on your neck and back muscles? The next time you are at a stoplight, take note of how many people are checking their phones. I didn't even mention the ones who are texting while driving.

I find people eating together at a restaurant to be particularly interesting. It never fails, technology is on the table or in hand and frequently checked by one or all parties. What's the impact of that on the relationship? What message are you sending? "Being with you is okay, but what's happening on Facebook is more exciting." I recently heard of a game someone plays when eating out with their friends: they put their phones on the table, and the first one to look at their phone has to pay the bill.

Oh, and do not be sneaky. Turn off those buzzes and beeps. If you are really worried about missing something important, some smartphones have a VIP feature. Calls from people on your VIP list will be able to ring through. Another thought that may help is to keep your phone out of sight. Sometimes, I leave it in the car or zipped up in my purse.

Personal Insight: What are you missing out on when you are constantly connected to your electronic leash? What adjustments are you interested in making to decrease the chance of being lured by your electronics?

Twenty-Five

JUST LIKE PAVLOV'S EXPERIMENTS

*R*esist the technology magnets by understanding why you feel drawn to them. It's human to want to feel liked or important. Pings and vibrations are signals to us that someone has reached out to us in some way. When we post on social media, we want to know if it was witty or inspirational enough for others to comment or "like." If they like our posts, then they like us. Now, of course, that's not how most of us think consciously, but subconsciously is another story.

Personal Insight: Spend a few minutes considering why you find it difficult to turn off your phone or its notification signals.

Twenty-Six

RE-CREATING THE WHEEL

*Y*ou are smart, innovative, and *busy*. Please do not re-create the wheel, trying to figure out problems when the solutions are at your fingertips. You can increase your productivity by networking with others. Ask friends and colleagues about helpful solutions they've found for concerns you are facing. There are certain tools and systems that others use that may streamline your processes. When you do ask, you are likely to find out about a number of services, productivity apps, websites, etc., that you didn't know about. On a similar note, before investing time and money, ask friends if they have had experience with these products and services.

> *Personal Insight: Paying bills, going through mail, deleting e-mails, cleaning, laundry, and meal preparation are just a few of many tasks that we trudge through. What areas of your life need an efficiency makeover? Who will you ask to help?*

Twenty-Seven

SPEND DEVOTED TIME WITH LOVED ONES

E-mails and phone calls do not count as spending time with someone. Spend time face to face. Laugh. Talk. Eat. *Together.* I live in a large metropolitan area, and many of my in-town friends live thirty minutes or more away. Due to our busy schedules (which include travel), one friend and I had to schedule out two months to get together for dinner! With another busy friend, we started scheduling back-up dates because too often there would be other competing agendas (a child's practice got cancelled, someone was sick, or a spouse had to travel). When you think about spending time with loved ones, don't forget about your children. Spending one-one-one time with children is necessary. When we run errands, my husband and I try to take one of our four children with us as one of the ways we build in quality time with them.

Personal Insight: Who do you want to spend quality time with? When will you schedule it? Once it is completed, write a brief note regarding the experience.

PERSPECTIVES: BALANCING ROLES

*A*s an entrepreneur, wife, and most importantly, busy mom, Tiffini shares her thoughts on balancing her multiple roles.

"My priorities are established daily. I don't put the people I love on the back burner. I may have to go somewhere for a work assignment, but often my children are right there with me. My husband may be taking the pictures that I post in the blog. This not only allows me to spend time with them, but it helps my family to understand what I do."

Twenty-Eight

WHEN YOU DO NOT KNOW
WHAT TO DO...
DO WHAT YOU KNOW TO DO

$\mathscr{S}$ ometimes, situations occur that leave us feeling confused, conflicted, powerless, and uncertain. When this happens, it's easy for panic and self-doubt to arise. Resist them. If you tell yourself you do not know what to do, you will believe it and act accordingly. You do not need to survey five people about your next move. Straighten your back and square your shoulders in preparation for dealing with it. Get quiet, pray, focus, and decide. Do not discount your power and abilities. Often you know what to do, but you allow panic and self-doubt to color your perspective.

> *Personal Insight: You have been steeped in and have absorbed wisdom, resources, and power. Act accordingly!*

PERSPECTIVES: BEING PRODUCTIVE

*J*ackie Brewton shares how she was able to be productive in other projects, even though she wasn't ready to complete her main project.

"I've been working on a book, for longer than I care to admit. It's been hard to complete it. I can be so disciplined in some areas and not in others. Instead of working on the book, I will come up with other great ideas. I finally decided that recording a DVD of a school assembly on the topic might be an easier task to accomplish in the short term. I was right! This summer, I released two DVDs, one for girls, and one for guys. You do not have to start with the hardest thing to get some success under your belt. Sometimes we make things more difficult than they need to be. In this case, I experienced some success and produced a great product, even though my book is not complete."

Twenty-Nine

BELIEVE THE BEST BEFORE YOU
BELIEVE THE WORST

*B*e optimistic. Your mindset affects your mood, energy, and even your health. Have faith in people. Believe that there really is good in the world. When you believe the best about people and situations, you encourage yourself, trusting that good things will come to fruition. When you possess this mindset, you look forward to the future. Your optimism not only brings out the best in you, but like a magnet it will draw other people to you and bring out the best in them as well. Believing the best has a ripple effect, and can positively touch every area of your life, including, personal, professional, spiritual, emotional health, and physical health. Believing the worst usually doesn't serve you well. It makes you defensive, hesitant, and closed-off. It is impossible to believe the worst and be in a positive mood. An enthusiastic outlook is good for the soul. You will experience less stress, increased energy, and will be more focused on the accomplishment of your goals.

Personal Insight: How has being optimistic served you well?

Thirty

PRESS UNTIL SOMETHING HAPPENS

*Y*ou are acting responsibly, ethically, and professionally—so what if you ruffle some feathers and step on some toes? Sitting quietly and waiting patiently for some gentle soul to make a path for you is not the most effective way to get what you need. You will not make a fool of yourself. PUSH—Press Until Something Happens—your way through the crowd. If the desire is great enough and you can imagine the possibility coming to fruition, get busy moving. It worked for the woman with the blood disorder who pushed through the crowd (Mark 5:25–34), and it will work for you.

> *Personal Insight: What do you want for your life so intensely that you are willing to push through a crowd to get it?*

Thirty-One

YOU HARVESTED WHAT YOU PLANTED

*D*id you know that if you plant tomatoes, only tomatoes will grow? Not green beans, potatoes, flowers, or anything else. *Only tomatoes!* This makes total sense in our literal gardens, but in the gardens of our lives, sometimes we are surprised by what we harvest. You were certain of what you planted until you saw what grew. Was something wrong with the seeds? Were you sabotaged? Are you really shocked that you got that performance rating with the level of work you put in? Were you genuinely taken aback when your friend said she didn't feel that you were there for her? You reap what you sow. Sow greatness to reap greatness!

Are your proverbial seeds falling on the sidewalk or among thorns? Are your seeds being planted in rocky soil, or have you taken the time to plant them in fertile soil? When your seeds have been planted in quality soil, they grow bountifully. The rocks and thorns in your life may be your environment, co-workers, family, or friends.

> *Personal Insight: Think about what results you want to harvest. What have you planted? Do you need more effort? Are there weeds you need to pull? Have you planted well? Check the soil, sun, and water. Is your work getting the proper nurturance? You must take good care of your seeds.*

Thirty-Two

NO SHORTCUTS

Turns out, your parents were right. There are no shortcuts in life. You cannot rush a quality product. When you cut corners, the results are mediocre. I prefer butter over margarine and sugar over artificial sweetener. Have you ever noticed that food grown in an artificial environment does not taste as good as food grown the old-fashioned way? I am not on a soapbox, but my point (besides a none-too-subtle agriculture lesson) is that your good thing is coming. It is particularly easy to cut corners when you are tired. You may get weary, but don't give up. Galatians 6:9 NIV advises, "Do not let yourselves get tired of doing good. If we do not give up, we will get what is coming to us at the right time."

Personal Insight: What is it that you are finding difficult to be patient for?

Thirty-Three

BELIEF MAKES ALL THE DIFFERENCE

*O*ur thoughts become our reality. When you believe you can accomplish your goal, your behavior lines up with your thoughts. When you believe, you prepare and execute with confidence. Olympic champions do not run races thinking they are probably going to lose. People who are successful at losing and maintaining weight loss believe they will be successful. Even if your belief falters briefly, refocus your thoughts and energy on your goals. Assistance from people who believe in you, as well as scripture, inspirational music or poetry, and other supportive resources may also help to recharge your belief in your ability to accomplish your goals. Have you heard the inspirational, against-the-odds stories of people like Tony Dungy, President Obama, and Oprah Winfrey?

> *Personal Insight: Make a list of what you will do to increase your belief in your own abilities. Start with making repeated, verbal statements of affirmation and belief to yourself.*

PERSPECTIVES: VISUALIZE. BELIEVE. EXECUTE.

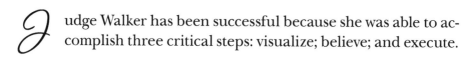

J udge Walker has been successful because she was able to accomplish three critical steps: visualize; believe; and execute.

Fourteen years ago, newly admitted to the Tennessee Bar Association, Allegra Montgomery Walker declared her intent to become a judge. In December 2013, Attorney Walker began her official quest for the judicial bench. Envisioning and believing that she would be victorious was foundational to her journey. There were considerable obstacles, but even when she had her moments of frustration, she never gave up. Allegra would joke that she couldn't quit her campaign run because she'd resigned from her job as assistant prosecutor to run for judge and didn't have another job. Quitting was neither an option nor a consideration.

Belief alone won't accomplish goals; preparation is critical. As a result of resigning from her position as assistant prosecutor, she had no steady income, nothing she could count on, no security. Although her husband worked, they had been a dual-income family. But Allegra had begun preparing in advance. She had paid off debt and positioned herself financially to be able to weather nine months of not receiving a paycheck. She stepped out of her comfort zone and stepped in to faith. She started with very little money and a lot of determination.

Overcoming obstacles requires grit and fortitude. "He has more money, but I have more hustle" is one of my favorite quotes from Allegra's campaign. The father of Allegra's opponent had been on the bench in the same court system for four terms (thirty-two years). Through his father's relationships, her opponent (who didn't have nearly the experience she had) secured a lot of endorsements and campaign donations. As a candidate, that's what you are supposed to do, so that was great for him. The required campaign disclosures revealed that Allegra's opponent had twice the amount of money as she had. Allegra seemed to be David, and her opponent was Goliath. Yet she was undeterred. Mark Twain once remarked, "It's not the size of the dog in the fight, it's the size of the fight in the dog."

Thirty-Four

360-DEGREE FEEDBACK

*D*o you listen to the feedback you get from others? Pay attention. It may be verbal or nonverbal, but you do receive feedback. The feedback you receive from family, friends, co-workers, colleagues, subordinates, and supervisors provides rich data about your strengths, weaknesses, and how you are perceived. You do not have to rely on your own interpretations; be direct and ask for specific feedback. You might ask their opinion of your leadership skills, approachability, or ability to solve problems. Ask them how much fun you are. What are their most vivid memories of you? Ask how effective they think you are at balancing personal versus professional demands?

> *Personal Insight: How can you use the feedback you receive to improve your success?*

Thirty-Five

BE EMOTIONALLY BALANCED

*B*eing emotional gets a bad rap. What's wrong with engaging your emotions? They are part of you; do not berate yourself for having them. Who would you be without your emotions? Our emotions are born out of the experiences that surround us. We are excited at good news, worried and saddened by tragedy, angered by injustice, curious about new things, proud of accomplishments, and embarrassed by mistakes. Everyone has emotions—they are natural and are not bad. However, we must learn to rule over our emotions and not be ruled by them.

In her *Dialectical Behavior Therapy*, Dr. Marsha Linehan notes the differences between reasonable mind, emotional mind, and wise mind. In *reasonable mind*, you view the world rationally and pay attention to observable facts and phenomenon. You may notice that you are in reasonable mind if you feel somewhat detached from the situation and find yourself noticing the facts and planning future behavior based solely on observable knowledge. In *emotional mind*, you may experience an intense subjective state wherein logical thinking becomes difficult or cloudy.

Neither emotional mind nor reasonable mind is bad. Operating with a balanced and integrated view of emotion and reason is the wise approach. We are human, so sometimes we operate there; sometimes we do not. When we live from a wise mindset, we can be effective in our actions and operate in our best interest.

Personal Insight: Think about the last time you had both feet in emotional mind or both feet in reasonable mind. In hindsight, what could you have done or what did you do to take a wise-mind position?

Thirty-Six

MEASURE TWICE, CUT ONCE

*H*ave you ever felt that you could not trust someone but were undecided on whether you should give them yet another chance? Have you determined that you need to leave your current job because your skills are being fully utilized and your pay is less than you deserve; however, you are uncertain what to do about the new job opportunity that has come your way? Make a well-informed decision and stick to it. You've thought about it. Talked about it. Prayed about it. *Now do it!* Plan your actions with forethought and consideration, then get busy. I like the saying, "Think long, think wrong." I also say, "If your thinking is too hazy, you'll drive yourself crazy!" Do yourself a favor and be decisive.

> *Personal Insight: Are you a talker or doer? You have made your plan; now when does it go live?*

Thirty-Seven

DO NOT EVER MEASURE YOUR SUCCESS AGAINST SOMEONE ELSE'S SUCCESS

*C*ompare yourself to yourself, not to other people. You haven't walked in their shoes, and they haven't walked in yours. How can you be a unique and special individual if you are exactly like someone else? You can't! Likewise, your journey can't be easily compared to the journey of others. Just because something works for them does not mean it will work for you. Your personality and goals are different from theirs. It's cool to look and admire. But decide if their technique fits you before you try to integrate what works for *them* into *your* life.

Line up your behavior with *your* goals, not your neighbor's. It's easy to become discouraged when you compare your accomplishments to the accomplishments of others. Runners do not look at the other lanes when they are racing because it will slow them down. The same goes for you. Looking at others too long will distract you and slow your pace. Once you have identified the goals and strategies that are custom-designed for you, you have all the resources you need to measure your personal success. You need not be concerned about those other folks.

Personal Insight: What tools do you use to measure your success?

PERSPECTIVES: PLEASANTLY DIFFERENT

*A*t times, it has required them to stand alone, but Pastor Veta, Dr. LeTosha, and Dr. Pam embrace being different.

Pastor Veta

"I don't worry about what people think about me as long as I'm kind to everyone. I don't worry about what people think of me as long as I know that my protocol falls in line with that of Jesus Christ. I'm not concerned about those other things. I don't try to dress like them. I don't try to act like them. Ultimately my goal is to please God, so if it makes me different, then I take pleasure in being different."

Dr. LeTosha

"Our life experiences make us special and different. My parents instilled in me to not follow the crowd. I don't want to be like anyone else. I don't want to look like other people. I don't want to listen to what they listen to. I was raised to have an independent mind. I was raised to follow my pathway. I don't want to—and I can't—travel other people's paths because those are not my path. In some regards, I've been ostracized. I've been called stuck up; I've been asked, 'Why do you talk that way? Why do you have that?' It can be painful at times. It's easy to be a conformist. It's hard to go against the grain. I've had to forgo some relationships. You learn that it's a path that has very few people."

Dr. Pam

"In high school, I was voted most likeable. That title haunted me! I felt like everyone should like me. I wondered and worried if they would be upset with me. As I matured, I realized It didn't matter if others accepted me. I had to be okay with me. I had to come to terms with who I was. Was I going to serve God or man? I had to stop worrying about other people."

Thirty-Eight

DO YOU HAVE A RUBBER BUTT?

*H*ave you ever had the experience of failing to meet a professional or personal goal? One of my goals is to be able to run a 5k without stopping. In my first attempt I did a combination of walking and running. Shortly afterward, I stopped training between races. My motivation declined and my excuses increased. I felt like a quitter and it disgusted me. In my heart, I knew I wasn't a quitter and I could run a 5k non-stop. I resumed running again and increased the number of days per week that I trained. I also ran with my children so that they could hold me accountable to my goal.

Success is often preceded by multiple failures. After a period of inactivity, I felt discouraged, but hearing the success stories of others encouraged me to keep trying. With repeated attempts to succeed, your strategy becomes more defined, your plans are more clearly articulated, and if it is something you are really passionate about, your drive is strengthened. Through your struggle, be encouraged. It is easy to let frustration, embarrassment, and fear become obstacles to you trying again. However, if you are truly passionate about accomplishing your goals you will continue to strive to meet your aspirations. George S. Patton said, "I do not measure a man's success by how high he climbs but how high he bounces when he hits bottom."

Personal Insight: Do you land with a bounce or a thud?
What success have you enjoyed because of your persistence?

Thirty-Nine

DO YOU LIVE BY FEAR OR FAITH?

*P*eople who live fearfully often take little steps or none at all. People who live by faith wisely take small, moderate, and huge steps. At times you will see them running, and—*look out!*—they leap too. The life on the inside of us will be visible on the outside. Are you surrounded by faith walkers or fear walkers? Know that their walk has the potential to influence yours.

Personal Insight: Do you leap with faith or freeze in fear? Why? What's the basis of your fear or faith?

Forty

DO YOU KNOW YOUR WORTH?

$\mathcal{F}$eelings of adequacy or inadequacy indicate how one emotionally evaluates their worth as a person. Thus, feelings of inadequacy occur when you devalue your worth and abilities. What you believe about yourself becomes a self-fulfilling prophecy. You can be successful according to this culture's standards and still have a very low and debilitating view of yourself. The ripple effect of this is significant. Feelings of inadequacy can negatively affect your relationships, cripple your creative and professional pursuits, and can have a devastating impact on your health. If this applies to you, consider journaling about your value and worth, ask others what they value about you, and/or consider going to therapy. Everyone has value. You have value even if you don't recognize it right now.

> *Personal Insight: Beliefs are powerful. Do your beliefs about yourself leave you feeling empowered and capable or weak and frustrated?*

Forty-One

WHERE DO YOU LIVE?

*D*o you live out of your strengths or your weaknesses? Are your thoughts consumed with the things you can't do and the people who are standing in your way? Or are your thoughts filled with positive expectations about what you are able to accomplish? It is normal to want to improve your weak areas, and you should. But don't neglect continuing to develop your areas of strength.

If you'd like to see what your character strengths are, you can take the free VIA survey at http://DrElahee.pro.viasurvey.org. There are tips at the site to show how you can exercise your character strengths.

> *Personal Insight: Think about the last few opportunities that came your way. Was your initial thought about how your strengths lined up with the opportunity or about how your weaknesses would impact the opportunity? Why do you think that was your reaction?*

Forty-Two

EVERYTHING LIVING HAS A LIFE CYCLE

*H*ave you ever tried to revive or keep alive something that was dead or dying? How'd that work out for you? Let it go. Say goodbye. Make room for new things, new life, new people, and new possibilities. Ecclesiastes 3:7 reminds us there is a season for everything. Sometimes people are afraid of letting go of things that have passed their expiration date. They fear moving on to new things, embracing instead the adage, "the trouble I know is better than the trouble I don't."

Personal Insight: What is it time to let go of?

PERSPECTIVES: DEALING WITH DISAPPOINTMENT

r. Pam grieved her infertility but now can share her insight on how she was able to let it go.

"When your plans and desires haven't come to fruition or do not line up with what God has for you, it can be a huge disappointment."

"I dealt with infertility for years. There was life before infertility and life after. In a way, this grew me up. I had just come to Christ a year before my infertility diagnosis. I learned that God prepares His children before they are about to hit the wall. When I got the news that I was infertile, it felt like somebody punched me in the stomach. I had enough of God's Word in me to be teased into going deeper. I had to go in search of this God who would allow this to happen to me. My fertility seemed contrary to His word. I prayed, 'Why would You not allow me to have a baby?' I come from a crazy family. I always said one day I'd have children, and it would be completely different from this."

"Why did God not let me have this childhood dream? I had two years of constant appointments. Fertility treatments. Labs. Medication. During this period, my mom had open-heart surgery, and my brother committed suicide. It was the craziest of times. After a couple of years, I decided I couldn't keep doing this. I was always focused on the next appointment, next lab, etc., to the point that I'd lost all joy in the present. If I was going to trust God, I had to put it all down. No matter how hard I might try to influence God, I couldn't. He is sovereign. When I was able to put this weight down, there was a release, a relief. Now this doesn't mean I don't have moments where I still desire to have children. I think, 'Wow. I don't have children. Who is going to take care of me when I'm elderly? Who is going to take me to get my hair fixed? Wipe my butt when I am ill and can't?' These moments are brief. Clearly God won't leave me out here to wallow. I have to constantly be mindful of trusting Him."

"When you desperately want something, it's easy to only see the benefits. It's a biased view. I began to see that it's a blessing to have children, but it could be a blessing not to have them as well. Motherhood is not promised to be a beautiful experience. When you're infertile, there is a tendency to only think about the good things you're missing. My mother aged exponentially when my brother's mental illness became full blown. My mother lived in fear of him."

Forty-Three

DO YOU RUN TOWARD CHALLENGES
OR AWAY?

*C*hallenges do not always feel good, but they do make you stronger—so embrace them. Your challenges are not going anywhere, so you may as well face them. To run from them will leave you conquered, feeling weak and doubtful. Decide that you will be the victor and add those challenges to your list of triumphs. As Pastor Veta says, "You gotta face it to fix it."

Personal Insight: How do you respond to challenges?

PERSPECTIVES: A NEW DAY

Jennifer Tacker

"It was November 2006, and I was staying at the Embassy Suites. The hotel is designed so that from every floor you can look down and see the courtyard. I was admiring the view and suddenly thought, 'It would feel so good to jump down there and die.' My next thought was, 'What the hell did you just say? Oh, hell no! I know I did not just think that!' That was my first clue that I wasn't myself. I was a miserable woman. My self-esteem was at rock bottom. I was overweight. I was wearing ponytails, and I had never worn a ponytail before in my life. I had two chemistry degrees and loved chemistry, but I hated my job."

Over the next two years, Jennifer waged war against her despair. She was prescribed antidepressants, hired a personal trainer, started seeing a counselor, strengthened her spiritual relationship with God through prayer and church, began journaling, and began a year-long job search. Also during this two-year period, Jennifer and her husband opened a restaurant with no prior experience. She learned that her spouse had engaged in multiple affairs—including her walking in on him cheating with someone she considered a friend and business partner. As a result, she separated from her husband.

As Jennifer committed to re-embrace life, she began to celebrate a series of hard-won victories. She lost over 130 pounds (going from a size 22 to a 10). Jennifer was offered a job that allowed her to engage both her love of chemistry and people, but the starting salary was $20,000 below the job she wanted to leave. Jennifer chose job satisfaction over money, reasoning that if she worked hard, she would be able to earn the additional $20,000 she was going to lose with the career change. Her fortitude proved fruitful. In the first year of her new job, Jennifer earned an additional $20,000 in commission and bonuses. The following year, Jennifer prayed about her ability to maintain the standard of living she and her children had been accustomed to while she was married. Then her prayers were answered. "I was getting coffee at McDonald's when my boss called," Jennifer says. "She told me I was getting a $21,000 raise!"

On a ten-point scale, Jennifer rated her level of life satisfaction in 2006 at a three. She was able to discontinue the antidepressants and therapy. Jennifer recalled, "I was out one night at this bar that had mirrors all over the place. I looked in the mirror, saw this face, and I thought, 'Who is that?' Then I realized—'That's me! and I'm pretty!'" By 2010, her level of life satisfaction was a ten.

Forty-Four

START WELL TO END WELL

*W*hat's the first thing you do in the morning? If you start your morning in chaos, your day is driven toward frustration and stress. If you start your day clearly focused and with a plan, there is a good chance your day will follow accordingly. Try starting your day quietly and peacefully, maybe in meditation or prayer, or by reciting positive statements about the day.

Personal Insight: Write the script for your perfect morning. How can you move closer to making this vision a reality? Choose one item from your list and make it part of your routine for the next week.

PERSPECTIVES: WINNING FORMULAS FOR LIFE

r. Pam and Dr. LeTosha have daily routines that are the springboards for the successful lives they enjoy.

Dr. Pam

"When it comes to my daily routine, I feel absolutely naked if I leave home without prayer! My morning routine varies depending on my schedule, but I wake at 4:45 a.m. for prayer and Bible study. I try to exercise and eat well. I don't eat fast food, and I don't drink soda. I'm not a purist; I just try to exercise some discipline. If I get ready to eat a piece of cake, I ask myself If I've already had sweets today. If the answer is yes, then I'm pretty good about not eating any more sweets that day."

Another vital aspect of Dr. Pam's life is to be actively engaged. "It is important for me to stay involved in learning and not to be boxed in by cultural standards. I am insatiably curious and love doing different things. As an adult, I've taken art, ballet, and ballroom dancing classes. People have tried to discourage me by saying, 'women don't…'; or 'black people don't…'; or 'you're already thin, why do you want to run a 10k?' But I pay them no mind, because I am clear on who I am living for."

Dr. LeTosha

"Prayer is definitely part of my winning formula. I have to have quality quiet time in the morning with God. Quality time means there is intimacy and communication with God. When there is intimacy (a deeper connection), His voice is more clear. When there is an overflow of His love from me to those around me, it is easier for me to give this overflow to others. I don't feel empty at the end of the day when I have had this intake exchange with the Father. It helps me stay balanced, which creates a more healthy me—mind, body, and spirit. When I have not spent quality time with God, I lose energy, and I'm not as patient, kind, or loving as I can be."

Forty-Five

MULTI-TASKING MISERY

*B*elieve it or not, you get more done when you focus on one task at a time. You dilute your effectiveness, waste time, and are more frequently distracted when you jump from one activity to another. Set stopping points based on progress or time, but eliminate going back and forth between tasks on a whim. Just because you think you can multitask does not mean it is a good idea. We've established that it does not increase your productivity, but it can also increase your stress and frustration levels.

Personal Insight: Have you experimented with mono-tasking? How did this work out?

Forty-Six

MINIMIZE YOUR "OPINION MINING"

*D*o you frequently ask others what they think about a decision you need to make? If so, stop…or at least slow down. Constantly inquiring about others' opinions about your work, wardrobe, ideas, etc., can make it appear to others that you feel inadequate and don't trust yourself. And if *you* don't trust your abilities, why should they? Have some confidence in your capacity to make the right choices for you. Also remember, when you get the opinions of others, you are not required to act on them. Consider it data, not a mandate.

> *Personal Insight: Do you find yourself opinion mining? If so, do you ask because you doubt yourself, or is there another reason?*

Forty-Seven

IMPROVING YOUR RELATIONSHIP
WITH YOUR SUPERVISOR IS
IMPERATIVE

*D*id you know your relationship with your manager is bidirectional? Managing your manager is mutually beneficial, because it allows you both to get what you need while benefiting the company overall. Your manager is not the enemy. Get to know his or her interests, concerns, work style, and priorities. Similarly, share your work style, goals, and concerns. This type of communication allows you both to be on the same page, and thus allows for improved communication and results with less frustration. By the way, this tip isn't restricted to your supervisor. It pertains to all your relationships.

> *Personal Insight: What would make your relationship with your supervisor better?*

Forty-Eight

YOU CATCH MORE BEES WITH
HONEY THAN VINEGAR

*I*f others are negative toward us, we are often quick to respond in like manner. Our tongues can be formidable weapons, wielding the capacity to cut others with our words in an effort to shut them down. Consider the personal cost of your actions. Imagine you are at a crossroads and have two choices. Choose an affable answer.

The benefits are for you, not them. "A gentle answer turns away wrath, but a harsh word stirs up anger" (Proverbs 15:1 NIV).

> *Personal Insight: Remember, particularly when you are feeling a little irritable, to respond in love and kindness. Doing so allows you to maintain your peace a little while longer.*

PERSPECTIVES: WORKPLACE EMOTIONS AND COMMUNICATION

Terri

There's an art to assertive communication, and Terri has mastered it like no one else I know. Terri is a public relations strategist who is ambitious, serious about her craft, and gifted with the ability to communicate with others in a clear and genuine manner. She is a straightforward, tell-it-like-it-is, tough-love kind of person who can say virtually anything effectively. Terri epitomizes the phrase "iron sharpens iron," and is a professional dedicated to truth, diligence, and motivation. In other words, she is the person you go to when you need to hear what you don't want to hear.

"When it comes to emotions in the workplace, stay on the side of professionalism. I try to remove emotion from the equation. I may come home and vent, but at work I stay strictly professional. I try not to take things personally. Sometimes it might be a personal attack, but then again, maybe it's not. It is all about how you receive things. I try to place everything in a business and professional context. It's critical that you care about how you perform your job, but when it comes to the behavior and personality of others, you can't be too tied to their emotional displays. The passion for my work that I bring to the job enables me to maintain my focus and it keeps me from being distressed by others.

"Similarly, with workplace communication, you shouldn't respond to a curt e-mail in an emotional way. You have to ask yourself what your goal is. What are you trying to accomplish? What is the desired outcome from this exchange? Remember to keep your focus on the work. As I said before, it is all about staying professional. When you have a strong work ethic, other people can see that. They know I'm not trying to be antagonistic because my passion for my work is evident. When your work product and professionalism are your focus, you build credibility, and others see you as authentic. That's how others will respond to you.

"Workplace drama is different from workplace politics. Office politics are about being strategic, understanding who the players are, and understanding their communication styles. People who think they have power communicate differently than people who are trying to gain power. Some of the players are trying to climb the ladder, and usually they are trying to prove they are the smartest in the room. They want to be smart, but they always have something for you to do. I manage these types of people by setting clear boundaries. Decision makers in the organization are also players in office politics. Rightfully so, decision makers feel accomplished.

They have a certain level of ego, but that doesn't mean they are egotistical. I try to manage expectations based on who I'm dealing with. Managing workplace politics is about having emotional intelligence. You have to manage people by having clear boundaries, being assertive, being comfortable with who you are, and understanding that you have earned your right to be there."

Forty-Nine

CONTINUITY IN RELATIONSHIPS

We've all heard it before. "Do not start behaviors in relationships that you can't continue for the duration of that relationship." This adage applies to work as well as personal relationships. Over time the dynamics of relationships can shift. Remember the way you used to be when you were first hired or first began a romantic relationship? There was an implicit agreement that you would continue to behave that way. If you want to see a positive shift in your work and personal relationships, go back to behaving the way you used to. Be kind, inquisitive, helpful, pleasant, arrive on time, and be reliable.

> *Personal Insight: In what ways have you moved away from the person you used to be? Why do you think that is?*

Fifty

WHAT ARE YOU WAITING FOR?

B ishop William L. Sheals said, "Stop expecting and start experiencing." Too often we become stagnant while waiting for something to happen. Don't just wait. Start behaving as though what you have been waiting for is happening *now*. If you were at a bus stop, would you not be looking down the street as if the bus was coming? Yes, because you're preparing yourself for when the bus comes and stops in front of you and opens its doors. You're not walking around starting conversations or on the other side of the street where there isn't a bus stop. You're in place, acting as if the bus is about to come. Do not just wait for it; behave as though you already have it. Experience it. Move in it. Dance in it. Plan in it. Do it. Still not sure what that looks like? Talk with authority. Walk with your head held high. Embrace an air of confidence.

> *Personal Insight: What are you waiting for? Will you recognize it when it arrives?*

Fifty-One

CHECK YOUR GAS GAUGE

*I*f your gasoline indicator light is on, that's your signal that you need to refuel. Exactly how far do you think you can get when your indicator panel says "0 miles"? Too many people try to optimize the fumes in their tank by trying to see how much further they can go on before their vehicle sputters to a stop. You have a lot of things to do and cannot possibly comfortably accomplish them if you're anxiously checking your gas gauge. Most of us refuel at regular intervals, but if you've logged more miles than usual by going to a few additional and out of the ordinary destinations, you will have to refuel sooner than you planned. Surely you can see the application of this analogy to your personal life. You have to refuel, otherwise you will run out of gas. Don't try to accomplish all that you have to do with an empty gas tank.

Another analogy is your emotional wellness checking account. Just being alive is an automatic withdrawal. Some activities withdraw larger amounts than others from your checking account. If you do not make deposits, you will have insufficient funds. Not sure what insufficient funds and an empty gas tank look like? Stress. Depression. Anxiety. Decline in spiritual relationship. Illness. Unhealthy relationships. Job dissatisfaction. To avoid these calamities, check your gas gauge and your account balance to be mindful of your current status. Make regular deposits to replenish what's been depleted.

> *Personal Insight: What signs and symptoms do you see in your life that tell you it's time to replenish? How will you replenish?*

PERSPECTIVES: WARNING SIGNS

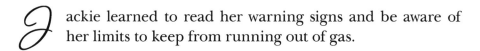

J ackie learned to read her warning signs and be aware of her limits to keep from running out of gas.

"When I am out of balance because I've worked too much, I start to do stupid stuff. There are warning signs. I lose focus. I have left the car running in the garage more than once. Sometimes I take a phone fast—no phone for a week except for business calls.

"To be balanced, I also had to come to terms with my limits. I had to face the fact that I couldn't do what I used to do and still fulfill my destiny. I had to let some things go. For example, for fifteen years, I faithfully sent birthday cards to family and friends. It got to the point that I couldn't keep up that pace. I had too many balls in the air, and they started to fall. That was also a warning sign. I had a friend who was hurt that after fifteen years, I'd forgotten to send her a card. I beat myself up a lot when I don't meet others' expectations. But I made a decision to let go of feeling like I was letting people down. I had to give myself permission to forgive myself and to come to terms with the fact that, if I was going to be successful, I couldn't add new opportunities without letting go of something."

Fifty-Two

GO WITH THE TRUTH

*W*hen you do not know what to say or how you feel and you're tempted to tell a "little lie," save yourself and your reputation. People respect people who are honest, even if they do not like the answer. Even if you are a nice person, others won't solicit your opinion for important concerns if your integrity has been found lacking. They believe you will tell them what they want to hear instead of what they need to hear. Your integrity is hard-earned. No one can maintain it but you.

Personal Insight: When are you most tempted to be dishonest? Why do you feel it's necessary to be dishonest? What purpose does that serve for you? Do you perhaps do it in an attempt to have others hold you in high regard?

Fifty-Three

ARE YOU STRUGGLING OR RESTING?

I hear people say that they are struggling to keep their faith in a person or a situation. When you have faith in a situation, you can let it go and proceed as though nothing is wrong. If you find that you are struggling, do something to address the issue. Have faith that the intervention will work. Monitor the intervention's progress with peaceful expectations. If the intervention does not work, fret not. Bishop William L. Sheals says, "Faith is not a struggle. Faith is rest and a way of life."

Personal Insight: Is your faith faux or restful?

Fifty-Four

STAY OUT OF HARM'S WAY

*D*o you play with lions, tigers, and bears? What about rabid dogs? Of course not! You protect yourself by keeping your distance from mammals that have the potential to harm you. From their stance and approach, you can read the aggressive behavior of four-footed mammals, yet you continue to find it difficult to read two-footed mammals, failing to see the passive aggressiveness and disingenuousness in people. Just as you wouldn't approach a wild animal, do not engage dangerous people. We describe people who have treated us poorly as people who have burned us. Similarly,

Proverbs 6:27 ESV questions "Can a man carry fire next to his chest and his clothes not be burned?" Consider it sage advice to limit your exposure to such people, "lest you learn [their] ways and entangle yourself in a snare" (Proverbs 22:24–25 ESV).

> *Personal Insight: Why do you find it difficult to avoid emotionally or socially dangerous people? Do you find it difficult to detect who they are? How are harmful people different from things you know to be harmful? How are they similar? What benefit do you get from interacting with them?*

Fifty-Five

DO YOU KNOW HOW POWERFUL YOU ARE?

The power to influence and help others is one of the greatest powers you possess. We are our brothers' and sisters' keepers. Just as we are impacted by others, others are impacted by us. Even if you do not notice them looking, trust me, they are. "In everything set them an example by doing what is good. In your teaching show integrity, seriousness" (Titus 2:7 NIV).

Personal Insight: How do you impact others? If you do not know, ask a few family members, co-workers, and friends for their opinions.

Fifty-Six

ARE YOU LIVING ACCIDENTLY OR INTENTIONALLY?

A ccidental living is reactive. Whatever happens, happens. You will clean up the mess and play the cards you are dealt. Intentional living is living with a plan, and that plan includes a contingency plan. You do not meander around aimlessly; rather you walk, talk, love, and have fun purposefully. And yes, for all the spontaneous people, you won't lose your spontaneity if you choose to live life proactively. A proactive approach to life decreases your unhealthy stressors. There are many other benefits as well.

> *Personal Insight: What benefits can you identify to living an intentional life? How does identifying these benefits influence your day-to-day life?*

Fifty-Seven

HOW STRONG ARE YOU?

*D*o you know signs of strength? We need to revisit the definition of what it means to be strong. Too many of my clients believe that sucking it up until you pass out, implode, or explode is a sign of strength. They have difficulty understanding that strong people ask for assistance when they need it. How ridiculous would it be for one person to carry a bulky and heavy piece of delicate furniture alone? Yet many of us look ridiculous, stumbling alone under the weight of our concerns and burdens.

Personal Insight: Complete this sentence: Strong women _____. Identify the qualities of strong women you know.

PERSPECTIVES: INNER STRENGTH

 r. LeTosha and Dr. Pam have discovered secrets to their strength.

Dr. LeTosha

"'I'm Every Woman' used to be my theme song! I have believed, known, and confessed that I am a strong woman. I can stand. I can persevere. I can endure.

"Recently, a test came along, and all of my endurance and even my faith was shaken. I felt weak. All I could do was to lay my whole self on God and the few people around me who were strong. I was so anxious, and I was fearful. I know God's Word, but I couldn't pray like I know to pray. I was facing blindness. I had so many fears: Would I be able to see? Would I be able to work? Would I be able to live? Who would take care of me? How would I be able to drive? Who will want me if I'm blind? I'm getting older. I've gained twenty pounds on this medication. The steroids I'm prescribed make me depressed, mad, and anxious. Yet, I knew the Word of God is in me. I knew that I know how to pray. I turned to my mother for support, laid every weight on her, and God brought me through.

"I have left the vast majority of the medical problems affecting my vision behind me. Through them all, God kept showing Himself strong. Every way was made for me. There was no financial delay, even though I had to be out of work. There were no surgery issues. I continue to be at a place of praying and believing and standing on the Word of God. I am learning that my point of strength is to get real low, as low as possible. When I'm not trying to bear all of the burden alone, I'm allowing God to be strong in my life. No more 'I'm Every Woman' for me. I can't be every woman. It's not all in me, as the song goes. I can't do it all on my own. Recognizing this makes me a strong woman!"

Dr. Pam

"A strong woman embraces her failures because they make her strong. You must come to terms with the fact that you are limited; you are not perfect. When a woman can face these truths, she is humbled and becomes more efficient. She no longer wastes time in the areas of failure."

Fifty-Eight

LIFE IS A DYNAMIC JOURNEY

*L*ife has its ups and downs. Murphy's Law reminds us that "If something can go wrong, it will." Regardless of this life truth, there's another truth. "Things can and will get better," if you stay the course. Just like spring, summer, autumn, and winter, our lives have seasons. Recalibrate and prepare for the continuation of the journey.

When I think about this point, bumper cars come to mind. Picture this: you are riding along having fun, and you are jarred by either getting bumped by someone else or bumping into someone else. Then you are on your way again until the next collision. In discussing her reaction to death, one of my coaching clients reflected that she was trying to adopt a more mature view of death by accepting that it is a phase of life, and although it's painful and sad, it's natural. Minister Queen Jackson eloquently put it this way, "Success is never final, and failure is never fatal." See Ecclesiastes 3:1–8.

> *Personal Insight: How do Minister Queen Jackson's words, "Success is never final, and failure is never fatal," impact the way you view your situation? If you can't apply it to anything you're going through right now, then what does it mean to you generally?*

Fifty-Nine

BEWARE OF DISTRACTIONS

*H*ave you ever been driving and been so consumed with what you saw around you that you missed your turn? It happens. If you are in a questionable neighborhood, you might be anxiously distracted. The more anxious you become, the more distracted you will be, which increases the likelihood of missing your turn. If you are in a pleasant environment and surrounded by beauty, you might be so relaxed and awestruck that you miss your turn. The nature of your distraction does not matter; the most efficient way to reach your destination is to maintain a healthy balance of vigilance. Be consciously aware—cautiously or pleasantly—and be focused on where you are and where your life GPS says you should turn, lest you hear the annoying "You have just missed your turn….Recalculating…Recalculating."

Personal Insight: Considering your destination, what are your likely (pleasant and unpleasant) distractions?

Sixty

YOU ARE SPECIAL BUT NOT INVINCIBLE

*Y*ou are a lot of things, but indestructible is not one of them. The health statistics are real. Heart disease, stroke, and other cardiovascular diseases (CVD) are the leading cause of death in American women, claiming over 400,000 lives each year, or nearly one death each minute. CVD kills approximately the same number of women as the next three causes of death combined, including all forms of cancer. It's easy to enact the stance of the three wise monkeys, Hear No Evil, See No Evil, and Speak No Evil. Unfortunately, doing so would be to your detriment. As women we spend so much time taking care of others, that we do not take care of ourselves. We feel like we can't afford to be sick, so we ignore the cues our bodies give that our system is not functioning at peak performance. Bottom line: Go to your physician and make sure your body is operating at its maximum potential. Your physician (who is a good candidate for your personal board of directors), should be someone that you trust and feel comfortable with. If your current physician does not fit this description, find another one.

> *Personal Insight: Do you get regular health evaluations? Do you follow the health recommendations you are given? Do you encourage the women around you to get regular health assessments?*

Sixty-One

GOOD NEWS—YOU ARE ONLY HUMAN!

*Y*ou are human, and that condition is not going to change anytime in the foreseeable future. As a result, you get everything that goes along with being human, starting with being imperfect. Hopefully, this reminder takes some pressure off of you. You do not have to be perfect to still be superb. You can make mistakes. You are improving—you will get better, you will mess up, and then you'll show even more progress. Do yourself a favor: stop condemning yourself for being human.

"We all stumble in many ways. Anyone who is never at fault in what they say is perfect, able to keep their whole body in check" (James 3:2 NIV).

> *Personal Insight: Rate yourself on a scale of one to five, with one being that you are underachieving and do not push yourself enough, and five being that you expect a lot from yourself and there is no room for error. Are there any adjustments you need to make in your expectations, beliefs, and behaviors?*

Sixty-Two

DO YOU KNOW HOW TO TURN UP
YOUR LEVEL OF LIFE SATISFACTION?

*T*here really are some things you can do to increase your life satisfaction. Research tells us that making a conscious effort to include more hope, zest, gratitude, curiosity, and love in our daily lives will lead to increased happiness and well-being. If you could do something to increase your level of happiness and life satisfaction, would you? Some activities that can improve your level of satisfaction with life are exercising, researching topics that interest you, and writing about good things that have happened throughout the course of the day.

> *Personal Insight: List the activities you will undertake in the areas of hope, zest, gratitude, curiosity, and love in order to improve your life satisfaction and well-being.*

PERSPECTIVES: 100 DAYS OF HAPPINESS

*D*uring one of the most tumultuous times in her life, Stephanie increased her level of happiness from a three to an eight on a ten-point scale in under eighty days. In the last two years, Stephanie has divorced her husband, moved away from her friends and beloved step-daughter, and suffered a considerable drop in income due to switching jobs. As she regroups, she notes,

"I never thought I'd move back to Cleveland, and I really never thought I'd move back to my mother's house." To say Stephanie was unhappy with her life would be putting it mildly. It was in the midst of this turn of events, however, that she was challenged by a friend to post daily thoughts regarding something that she was happy about that day.

She took on the challenge with a few reservations. Stephanie is a private person, and she is not one to post regularly on Facebook. It was difficult to get into the discipline of posting daily. To top it off, some people unfriended her on Facebook. "I felt bad initially, then I realized they didn't need to be my friends if posting about what made me happy for the day annoyed them. It is easy to focus on the negative. It gives us permission to complain. Misery loves company. When we talk about the negative, it's like saying 'feel bad for me.' There is satisfaction when others commiserate. Focusing on the positive has caused me to change my attitude and my perspective about my day. Positive energy is contagious. You get back what you give out."

One impact that is difficult to measure is how her challenge inspired others. "People inbox me all the time about me being an inspiration to them. I had no idea that it would be a benefit to others, and that's just the feedback I've received. I imagine there are people who have been impacted who have not in-boxed me. My resting face used to be a scowl. Now I smile all the time." She laughs at herself in amazement. "People who smiled all the time used to annoy me." Stephanie notices that smiling and keeping an upbeat attitude not only has had a positive impact on her mood and outlook, but it has impacted her co-workers. People who never smiled or greeted her before have begun to reciprocate the kind greetings. As a result of the benefits she has realized during this challenge, Stephanie plans to continue to do it daily, though most likely in a journal format instead of a social media outlet. Through this process, Stephanie's healing and happiness have also been aided by "spending time with friends, time with family, and spa days, spa days, spa days!"

Sixty-Three

WHO ARE YOU?

When asked to talk about yourself, how do you respond? Many begin by describing their occupation or other life roles, but is that who you are? I recall being in a group setting with a colleague who'd emigrated from Japan a few years before. We were all to pair up, spend a few minutes getting to know each other, and then introduce our partner to the group. My Japanese colleague introduced his partner by commenting on the person's character instead of introducing his partner's roles in life.

It's common for people who lose their jobs to feel disconnected with who they are. If you are not sure how closely your identity is tied to your degree or job title, imagine living life without it. Mentally strip away those elements one at a time. When do you feel most vulnerable? That may be a clue as to which identifier means the most to you.

Personal Insight: How closely is your identity tied to your career? Who are you without those identifiers?

Sixty-Four

THE PHYSICS OF BEHAVIOR

Undoubtedly you have heard that the best indicator of future behavior is past behavior. There is one caveat—things are likely to stay the same unless there is a strong outside intervention. We learned this in physics class, right? Recall Newton's First Law of Motion: "An object in motion stays in motion with the same speed and in the same direction unless acted upon by an unbalanced force." Simply put, the past is not always indicative of the future if someone has had a life-altering, one-hundred-eighty-degree turn-around. We've heard the stories of former criminals, substance abusers, and batterers who have been reformed. Of course, it's not always prudent to believe one's "trust me; I've changed" declaration. They need to show, not just tell, you about the changes, but change can happen.

> *Personal Insight: How can you maintain a stance of optimistic self-preservation toward people who have burned you in the past?*

Sixty-Five

ONE-SIDED RELATIONSHIPS
DO NOT WORK

I was being interviewed to participate in a program with senior citizens. The director asked me what I wanted to get from my relationship with the senior citizen I would be matched with. I was thinking about the relationship I enjoyed with my own grandparents and wanted to be of assistance to a senior citizen in need. Thus, my response was "Nothing. I don't need anything." I was enlightened yet surprised when the director replied, "A relationship that you expect nothing out of will not be a successful one. You'll get tired of giving and not receiving anything back. Eventually, you'll withdraw from; or become irritated with the senior. Maybe you want the senior to share stories with you, to teach you to play bridge, or how to garden. You do not have to want much, and it does not have to be tangible, but you have to get something from the relationship for it to work. Personal relationships should be mutually beneficial." Sage advice.

Personal Insight: Are your relationships lopsided or mutually beneficial?

Sixty-Six

TRUST YOUR GUT

We hear it a lot, but trusting your intuition is not as easy as it sounds. A lot of noise comes our way from television, radio, computer, tablet, cell phone, friends, family, church, community, and work…the list does not stop. Quiet yourself and your environment so you are able to focus on what your body and your mind are telling you. What feels right? Do you not have time for reflection and introspection? Your brain is processing details, remembering, and analyzing more facts than you can keep up with yourself. You do not get the transcript; rather, it's the bottom line that registers. Trusting your gut often boils down to going with the summary of your senses. John 16:13 NIV reads, "But when he, the Spirit of truth comes, he will guide you into all the truth. He will not speak on his own; he will speak only what he hears, and he will tell you what is yet to come."

> *Personal Insight: When has trusting your intuition proven to be in your best interest?*

Sixty-Seven

SAY "THANK YOU"

S aying thank you is priceless. Do not just say it; mean it. Feel it. When you do that, the recipient will feel it too. I get excited when I receive good customer service. I have even been known to seek out managers to tell them how wonderful an employee is. I get annoyed, however, when salespeople automatically mutter, "thank you, come again," and hand me my purchase without even looking at me. When someone does something for you, even if it's the smallest of considerations, pause and thank them with meaningful words. It will positively impact you and them.

> *Personal Insight: Today, be conscious of your expressions of gratitude.*

PERSPECTIVES: GRATITUDE

r. LeTosha, Dr. Pam, and Pastor Veta discuss the value of express-ing gratitude.

Dr. LeTosha

"When you say thank you, I want to do all I can for you. It's be-ing gracious. It's showing love. Saying thank you can be disarming. It can melt you. I gave a child a shot, and she looked at me with tears in her eyes and said, 'Thank you.' I caused her discomfort.

What I was doing to her didn't feel good to her, but she knew it was necessary. In her pain, she was able to thank me. It's an extremely powerful phrase."

Dr. Pam

"I heard a pastor say that a thank-you is a prayer in and of itself. Every time you say thank you, it is an acknowledgement of your gratitude and your being humbled. It pierces people's hearts in a subtle way. It's paying tribute to someone else, acknowledging and edifying the receiver. A thank-you enriches others.

"Some people have difficulty accepting a thank-you. I tell people who have a hard time receiving a compliment to just be quiet, because when you continually deflect compliments instead of accepting them graciously, people begin to treat you as though you don't have value. They don't do this deliberately; rather, it occurs subconsciously. When you dismiss compliments and devalue yourself in front of others on a regular basis, people slowly get to the point where they don't bother to go there with you anymore. You become invisible. Having difficulty receiving a thank-you is an issue of self-worth."

Pastor Veta

"One of the things I like to teach people is that they should treat themselves like they treat others; that's if they treat people well. If you compliment others, compliment yourself. As women, we put forth every effort to look good before we step out the door. We want people to pay us compliments, but for a lot of women, as soon as someone does pay them a compliment, they say, "Oh, this old dress? I've had this thing for ten years," instead of simply saying, "Thank you." It's really a false humility because you know you put forth the effort to look good—but then it's so hard to accept that compliment. I have had to teach myself to say thank you. I appreciate compliments because I know from whence I came. When someone tells me I look nice or I look just like a lady, my mind goes back to the fact that I was not raised by a mother; God taught me how to be a lady. So when people give me that compliment, I tell them thank you because the glory goes to God.

Sixty-Eight

THE ROAD NOT TAKEN

S ometimes in life we reach a crossroads. The conundrum of choosing the correct path is not always crystal clear, and it can be pretty troubling. There is a popular poem by Robert Frost that reflects on his journey in the woods. He came upon a split in the road and realized that, as much as he desired to travel both, he had to choose one. But how would he choose? Both roads looked desirable and equally worn. Forced to choose only one road, he imagined how he would tell the story of his journey. He mused that he would sigh, saying that he made the wisest decision, choosing the road less traveled.

I often advise clients in a similar position to just pick one. We fear that there will be significant adverse consequences down the road, but we have no idea what they might be. We never really know what awaits us. Just hold your breath and jump into the deep end of the pool. Stop stressing over what you may have missed. As with Frost's poem, you will never know what you missed because you can only travel one road. Trust that your destiny will unfold just as it should and that all the lessons you needed for growth and all the opportunities for prosperity were available on both roads. Simply put, you can't go wrong with either choice. Romans 8:28 NIV reminds us that it all works out in the end: "And we know that in all things God works for the good of those who love him, who have been called according to his purpose."

> *Personal Insight: What choice have you made that you are now second guessing? What will help you to finally let it go?*

Sixty-Nine

SOMETIMES, OLD-FASHIONED IS BEST

There are times when a phone call or a face-to-face meeting is necessary. Texting, e-mailing, in-boxing, posting, and all the other ways one might communicate via technology just won't cut it. When you need to have a sensitive or complex conversation or if you want to grow a relationship, then make the call or make an appointment to meet in person. In electronic communication, there is too much room for misinterpretation. There is a lot to be said for voice inflection and the instant give-and-take of a conversation.

> *Personal Insight: Have you ever sent or received an electronic communication that went wrong? What lessons did you learn? How was the relationship impacted?*

Seventy

WHAT EXCITES YOU?

Too many times, I coach women who have reached an impasse in their life. When queried about what they used to enjoy in life, too many people have difficulty recalling these memories. Maybe it was painting, running outdoors, or cooking…if you still can't recall, then it's time to rediscover. Take classes. Try new things, both alone and with friends. Try activities that you've been curious about and activities that you thought you'd never do.

Personal Insight: Rediscover your interests.

Seventy-One

WHEN EXACTLY?

*H*ave you ever seen the words *someday* and *soon* on a calendar? If you have, please forward a copy to me. *Someday* and *soon* are both adverbs that reference an undefined period of time. If these words are in your vocabulary, then you are most likely trying to avoid or delay a goal. Are you unprepared for it, or do you just not want to do it? One of the worst things you can die with is potential. Die with failures before you die with potential. Potential is something to be realized, not guarded and protected. Dr. Henry Cloud advises you to "get your potential on the calendar under an identifiable month, day and year, not buried under a 'someday' or 'soon.'"

> *Personal Insight: List your somedays and soons. Either put a date next to them or put "I do not know." The clearer your language, the better for you and those around you.*

Seventy-Two

HOW COMFORTABLE ARE YOUR SHACKLES?

For some, the response to uncomfortable shackles is instant, especially if the shackles are painfully tight. Too often, however, we get used to the discomfort, and it becomes part of daily life. We continue to allow our circulation to be cut off and our mobility to be restricted.

Others of us are held captive by soft, comfy shackles. They are still shackles, but they are deceptive because they are cute or comfortable. We overlook the restriction and discomfort because of the compliments we receive or because we enjoy the bling or coziness. Shackles do not have to be metal cuffs and chains; they can be anything—poor health, a nice paying job, a loved one whose feelings you do not want to hurt, a house you can't afford or do not want to live in anymore. Typically, you can identify your shackles because you are not where you want to be or you make excuses for why you haven't done something different.

> *Personal Insight: List your shackles. You have the key, so what keeps you bound?*

Seventy-Three

ARE YOU STAGNANT IN YOUR GOALS?

On the line provided, identify the reason that you are not reaching your goals: _____.

No, it's not a misprint. The line is that size for a reason. How much space do you need to write "me"? Do not get discouraged. There is a way in, a way over, a way under, a way below, and a way through. If you're unsure of one way, go the other way. Notice that action on your part is required and will not come floating through the window, to land gently on your lap.

Personal Insight: How are you doing in the way of your goal attainment?

Seventy-Four

DO NOT UNDERESTIMATE THE
BENEFIT OF A GOOD FIRE

*C*an you identify the benefits of fire? Did you know that fires can be healthy? Naturally occurring forest fires reduce dead vegetation, stimulate new growth, and keep the forest from getting too dense and overgrown. A healthy forest will to continue grow even after a fire. Similarly, there are two Chinese symbols that are used to describe a crisis: danger and opportunity. For some, a fire is a crisis. See your fire as not only dangerous but as an opportunity.

Personal Insight: What seems like a natural disaster in your life may actually be a mechanism for clearing out useless hindrances. What have proverbial fires made a clearing for in your life? What opportunities have come out of your crises?

Seventy-Five

PUT YOUR MONEY WHERE YOUR
MOUTH IS

*W*hen did you last purchase clothes, accessories, a purse, or shoes? How often do you treat yourself to lunch or dinner? What about your beautifully styled hair? Review your debit or credit card statements to determine how much you have spent on these items in the last six months. I understand needing to make these purchases. We have to eat, right? After all, we can't risk becoming ill due to malnourishment. Furthermore, as long as we are legally required to wear clothes, we may as well look good in them! Now that you are sated and looking fine, ask yourself if you have also spent money on things that will enhance you spiritually, mentally, physically, or emotionally? Have you purchased things that will add to your well-being?

I have seen women complain about the cost of a $500 weekend retreat focused on spiritual, emotional, financial, and interpersonal growth, but they have no concern over purchasing a $500 purse or outfit. The same women will then complement the $500 indulgence with shoes and dinner. Matthew 6:21 reminds us that wherever we place our treasure, our hearts will be there also.

> *Personal insight: When is the last time you invested in yourself in a substantial way? What it would take for you to invest in yourself regularly and in a meaningful way?*

Seventy-Six

PURGE

*A*ccumulation of "stuff" such as clothes, mail, and items you no longer have use for occurs easily. However, inevitably, one day you look around and realize that you feel crowded by your "things" and are unable to grow. It is then that you realize, some of these things must go. In your assessment, you recognize that some things are broken, never worked well, and no longer fit your needs. Similarly, there are some people and situations that you need to be free of for your own benefit. Do you have people in your life who seem to take away from your life more than they add? Are you associated with people who seem to be going in the opposite direction as you? Remove them from your life completely and efficiently as possible. Some examples may include, declining their invitations and not accepting their phone calls. Every situation is different so confide in someone who can help you strategize on the best plan. If your answers to these questions refer to people who you can not easily get rid of such as a parent of supervisor, try to spend less time around them and definitely do not invest what is precious to you with them. For example, if your mother is emotionally toxic, she is not the person you should share your hopes and dreams with. (If the relationship you need to purge is abusive, please seek professional help first. For example, when a woman leaves an *abusive* relationship, she is most vulnerable.)

Dr. Henry Cloud, in *Necessary Endings*, describes three reasons to purge.

» It/he/she may be good but not best for you.
» It's a bad situation that is not going to get better.

» It's horrible, useless, and should have been gone a long time ago.

> *Personal Insight: Given these three scenarios, what are the thoughts, people, and situations that you need to purge from your life?*

Seventy-Seven

REMEMBER THE TORTOISE
AND THE HARE

S low and steady wins the race. How many changes are you trying to implement? Master one before you go on to another. Take your time—you do not need to do a complete life overhaul in one fell swoop. Even if it feels urgent, you can't implement a new exercise regimen, do a nutritional makeover, undertake a path of self-discovery, and send daily gratitude letters all at the same time!

Personal Insight: Put your goals and life upgrades on a schedule and pace yourself.

Seventy-Eight

ARE YOU A LOVER?

*L*ove is a verb. It is a way of behaving, not merely an emotional feeling. It is something you do, and it shows up in the way you act. "Love is patient, love is kind. It does not envy, it does not boast, it is not proud. It does not dishonor others, it is not self-seeking, it is not easily angered, it keeps no record of wrongs. Love does not delight in evil but rejoices with the truth. It always protects, always trusts, always hopes, always perseveres" (1 Corinthians 13:4–7 NIV). I often think of love as a feeling, so reading this is a reminder to myself when I fall off the love wagon, that I have got this love thing all wrong. I refocus, and it lasts a little while longer…at least until the next time I fall off the wagon.

> *Personal Insight: How can you put your love into action?*

Seventy-Nine

WHAT'S ON YOUR PLATE?

$\mathcal{E}$ ver been in front of a scrumptious buffet and discovered that there is not enough room on your plate for everything you want to eat? Maybe you have a moment of indulgence in which you contemplate getting a second plate so you can enjoy it all. I hate to be the bearer of bad news, but you have only one plate, and it's not getting any bigger. There are only twenty-four hours in a day—always has been and always will be. If your plate is full, you must take something off before you put something else on it.

However you choose to get it off, you must be sure that you have a space for new additions.

> *Personal Insight: Draw a picture of a plate (or on your computer, insert a pie-chart diagram). Write in what's on your plate.*

Eighty

BUSY BUT EFFECTIVE?

$\mathcal{I}$ t's easy to find ourselves going full steam ahead like a freight train, when sometimes we don't have a set destination in mind. Sometimes we look at our lives, and it seems that our days are full of work, responsibility, and a few food and rest stops. You have being busy down to a science, but are you being effective? Are you making a dent in anything? Do you see progress toward your goal? Do you have a goal? Are you connecting with people on a deeper level as you zip from one activity to another?

    Personal Insight: How can you measure your level of effectiveness?

Eighty-One

IS THERE VALUE IN YOUR WORDS
AND ACTIONS?

*I*f you always say yes, your yes means nothing. People know you say yes to everything. But, if you say no sometimes, then when you say yes, your response will be more respected. If you join every group or ministry, you appear indiscriminate. But if you are selective, you appear more discriminating.

Personal Insight: Do you have a standard way of responding that may unintentionally undermine your credibility?

Eighty-Two

WHERE ARE YOUR BOUNDARIES?

Why should others respect your boundaries? They do not know where your boundaries are. Do you know where they are? Effective boundaries are marked and identifiable. Poorly enforced boundaries are ineffective. Have you ever seen a closed but unlocked gate or a chain that droops so low that you can easily step over it? These are poor boundaries that will be frequently disregarded. Setting clear boundaries allows you take care of yourself by making yourself a priority. Boundaries also serve as inspiration to others. People respect people who respect themselves. An example of a boundary is "No work calls after 6:00 p.m."—unless, of course, your job requires you to be on call. Please do not get fired. Such a boundary informs people that you separate your work life from your personal life. This may inspire them to take similar actions in their lives. Remember, no one can take care of you better than you can. And assuming you are an adult of sound mind, it is nobody else's responsibility to take care of you.

Personal Insight: Have you identified your boundaries, and are they clearly identifiable by others?

Eighty-Three

IF MONEY WEREN'T AN ISSUE...

What would you do for others if money weren't an issue? If you had no financial restrictions, what would you do for others? Would you provide school supplies for children who had none? Would you tutor someone or perhaps feed the homeless? Maybe you would help new mothers or take seniors to their appointments or to the grocery store. Identify who you would help, the resources you would need, who would assist you, time limits for the project, and why you want to do it. Many great ideas designed to serve others, began with little or no financial investment. So what's holding you back? You have gifts and resources. Imagine what would be possible if you shared your gifts with others. One of the things that makes life special is when people unconditionally and selflessly give to help others.

> *Personal Insight: Without money, what small step will you make toward your idea?*

Eighty-Four

DO YOU HAVE RIGID BELIEFS?

We do not like to admit it, but at some point, everyone has made a negative judgment about another group of people. You may wonder—if we have all done it, what's the harm in being judgmental? When we take this stance toward another, we shut down our ability to find out new and contradictory information that has the power to uproot our negative judgments.

Being judgmental also serves another purpose. It can be a way to deny your vulnerability and ability to be just like the group you have formed the negative judgment about. This position seeks to thwart the thought that that person could easily be you, and can be a way to ease your discomfort around another group. Lastly, the source of your disposition could be that secretly you are envious of them.

> *Personal Insight: Think about a group you have firm, unshakable beliefs and opinions about. What is at the root of that judgment? Where did it originate?*

Eighty-Five

WHAT HAPPENED TO YOUR GOALS AND DREAMS?

*A*re your goals and dreams alive and well, or are they in a coma? What myths and excuses are you believing that keep you from pursuing your plans? Did you get so busy in your life's roles that you forgot about your dreams? The difference between you and those people who followed their goals and dreams is that when they tripped over a hurdle, they got back up. Before you can follow your goals and dreams, you must make a plan. Habakkuk

2:2 NKJV admonishes, "Write the vision and make it plain on tablets, that he may run who reads it." How do you expect your dreams to become reality tomorrow if you do not have a plan? I read an interview of an actress who reflected on her divorce saying, "I divorced him because he didn't make me happy. A few years later, I realized even I didn't know what made me happy. If I didn't know, how could he?" Your goals and dreams are not restricted to your educational and career goals. The same principle applies to every area of your life.

Personal Insight: What did you stop dreaming about?
What were/are your plans for your goals and dreams?

PERSPECTIVES: YOUR VISION

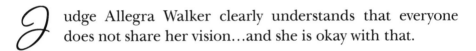

*J*udge Allegra Walker clearly understands that everyone does not share her vision…and she is okay with that.

When asked how she dealt with the negativity of others during her campaign, Judge Walker responded, "Their negativity gave me energy. I was in a spiritual place where I was guided by a higher power. It gave me an extra charge to prove others wrong. Negativity from others made me work that much harder. Sometimes it drove me to put in another 2-3 hours of work." Repeating a quote she'd read recently, Allegra notes "the dream is free. The hustle is sold separately." Adding, "people dream all the time but they don't want to put the work in. I had a vision, a dream for my future but it required me putting in work to make it come true. I wasn't going to be derailed by people who didn't have the same vision I had."

The morning following the election, Allegra and I were in her kitchen enjoying breakfast. Her phone buzzed, announcing another laudatory message. A text from her skeptical associate read, "Congratulations, I didn't think you could pull it off." How many people would have been angered or offended to receive such a message? Allegra's response was laughter! There were two important life lessons demonstrated in that brief moment: Keep your sense of humor; and understand that your vision does not have to be their vision.

Eighty-Six

THE CRAVING WHISPERER

W hen we get a craving for something, we will stop at nothing to satisfy it. Understand where your craving comes from. If you crave a candy bar, is it because you saw a commercial, skipped breakfast, or is it mood based? If you crave being alone, are you avoiding conflict, or do you have a lot to think about? When you crave, think about why you have that feeling. It's your body's way of telling you something needs attention.

Personal Insight: What do you crave?

Eighty-Seven

ARE YOU VULNERABLE?

We tend to cover up our weak areas. If we have an injury, we cover it with a bandage to protect it from further injury. Broken bones are covered by a cast. Similarly, we have internal vulnerabilities, ones that are not visible from the outside. We are usually more vigilant in covering unseen vulnerabilities than we are visible ones. We don't mind you knowing that we had a bad case of the flu, but we'll do everything in our power to hide that we are lonely, depressed, and afraid. We try to communicate to others that everything is great when, in fact, we are falling apart.

When you hide and deny vulnerabilities, you are not only protecting yourself from possible injury, you're also preventing assistance and help. Furthermore, when you maintain that all is well with you and things have never been better, not only do you reduce the likelihood that you will get help, you also increase the chances that *I might ask you* for assistance! Lastly, you cannot take effective care of yourself if you maintain the tough-as-nails, all-is-swell façade. Not only is that exhausting, it's a sure way to guarantee that your condition won't change anytime soon.

> *Personal Insight: Are you hiding your vulnerabilities or facing them head on?*

Eighty-Eight

FRIENDS

*Y*ou can't underestimate the value of a good friend. With friends, you can share your 'not-so-politically correct' thoughts and feelings without fear of judgment or reprisal. In your darkest, saddest, and angriest moments you can call each other, sometimes just to listen to each other, commiserate, laugh, or to say "You were wrong for that."

I have some *really* great friends. They provide insight, love, support, and challenge me. One friend is particularly dear to me because she helped me during a tough period in my life when I was angry and hurt about the addiction and subsequent incarceration of a close family member. I blamed this family member for the emotional impact his decisions had on our family. I was angry that he seemed not to care how his behavior affected his loved ones. My friend allowed me to vent without judging me. Later, when I was ready, she sympathized with me, and eventually told me, "Girl, it is time to let that go." Her counsel allowed me to see how holding onto anger was having a deleterious effect on me. That experience helped me realize that I can accept people as they are without accepting their behavior.

Personal Insight: How do your friends make you better? How can you be a better friend?

Eighty-Nine

SELF-CARE FOR THE SOUL

*W*hen our loved ones are having a difficult time, we are loving and tender toward them. We hug them and speak comforting, encouraging words; we assure them that everything will be okay. However, when we experience the same issue, too often we respond in a completely different manner. Gone are the comforting words of self-assurance. Instead, we beat ourselves up or tear ourselves down. When we experience difficult times, we should be as loving to ourselves as we are to those we love.

>*Personal Insight: In what ways can you be more loving and understanding to yourself when you are going through a difficult time?*

PERSPECTIVES: HYPOCRISY

*P*astor Veta wants to be aware of her own hypocrisy.

"This may be a strange statement, but one of my self-checks is that I can hear my hypocrisy when some things come out my mouth. We encourage so many people. We give them advice. For instance, I'll fuss at folks for missing a doctor's appointment when I haven't even made mine. I'll fuss at people for criticizing themselves, when sometimes in my own mind, I'm critical of myself. I often pray, 'God, let me hear the hypocrisy before it comes out of my mouth.'"

Ninety

FORGIVENESS

orgiveness is good for the soul. For some issues and some people, forgiveness can happen instantly. For others, forgiveness is a process. When you do not forgive, you remain trapped by your issue. Too often we want to be forgiven, but we are reluctant to forgive. It is important that we "be kind to one another, tenderhearted, forgiving one another, even as God in Christ forgave you" (Ephesians 4:32 NKJV). Unforgiveness is a weight. It is hard to maneuver with a weight on your back.

> *Personal Insight: Who do you need to forgive? How has unforgiveness been a weight on you?*

Ninety-One

THE BLAME GAME

We all mess up sometimes, and when we do, it's really tempting to get defensive and blame others. In psychology, we talk about *attribution theory*. When a negative event happen to us, we blame external factors and deflect the blame from ourselves. When a negative event happens to someone else, we are more likely to blame that individual. When you find yourself getting defensive and placing blame, *stop*. Accept and own your contribution. "I apologize. I made a significant error, and I recognize the impact it has had on [insert the victim]." Next, explain how you will avoid repeating the error in the future.

> *Personal Insight: Do you find it tough to accept respon-*
> *sibility when you know that others have contributed to the*
> *error or have made errors that seem bigger than yours?*

Ninety-Two

BANISH THE BLAHS

Sometimes, days unceremoniously spill one into the next; they become bland and predictable. If you want to shake out of this drab routine, wear bright colors, take a different route to work, change your perfume, switch hairstyles, or watch comedy. The possibilities are endless. Do you always eat lunch at your desk? Go outside and get some fresh air. Whatever you are doing, if you are in a rut or going around in circles, make a deliberate change.

Personal Insight: There is a saying, "The trouble I know is better than the trouble I don't." Ruts are comfortable because they are predictable. Make a list of the benefits you will receive by climbing out of your rut.

Ninety-Three

IT'S WRITTEN ALL OVER YOUR FACE

*Y*our mood is reflected in your expression, and it has the power to infect and affect those around you. Have you ever been impacted by the warm smile of a stranger? Conversely, have you ever been impacted by someone's sneer and scowl? Something as simple as a genuine smile can completely shift your mood and the mood of others.

Personal Insight: Make a list of some of the things you can do to shift your mood to a positive one. Playing a favorite song or calling a friend who always makes you laugh are some examples.

PERSPECTIVES: LOOKING GOOD

*W*hen Dr. LeTosha is going through a tough time, she refuses to let it show.

"You don't have to look like what you're going through. You don't have to wear your situation externally. You don't have to tell everything, and you shouldn't always present a negative front. If you are going through a bad situation, don't wear browns and blacks and no makeup as though you were in mourning. If you are feeling bad, change your routine. It helps to draw new things to you in order to challenge the negative in your life. You are creating an atmosphere where you are receiving what you present. Wear bright colors and perfume. Smile. How you go through your situation is a testimony."

Ninety-Four

A FUNNY KIND OF MEDICINE

L aughter is exceptionally good for you. It can lower your blood pressure, reduce stress hormones, increase the response of your immune system, and improve memory, learning, and alertness. Laughter can release endorphins, the natural painkillers that promote an increased sense of well-being, and neuropeptides that help fight stress and potentially more serious illnesses. Laughter isn't just good for you; it's enjoyable. Laughter is relaxing and increases bonding with others. It's easy to do, and it's free. Proverbs 17:22 ESV says, "A joyful heart is good medicine," so laugh often!

>*Personal Insight: How can laughter be a larger part of your daily life?*

Ninety-Five

HAVE YOU BEEN TYPECAST?

*Y*ou are so much more than what others think you are. Do not limit yourself to the script. My brother-in-law is a minister, and at a recent family reunion, he endured a little good-natured ribbing for going down the Soul Train Line. Now, if he restricted his behavior by what others thought was permissible, he'd be a bored fly on the wall. Maybe you've been typecast as shy, quiet, mean, class clown, nerd, etc. Break out of your mold by doing something different and doing it well. Show your versatility.

    Personal Insight: How have you been typecast? Do you typecast others?

Ninety-Six

HELP WANTED

*H*as anyone ever helped you out of the kindness of their heart? Maybe you didn't know you needed help until their intervention. We are here to be of service to others—not just the downtrodden or your friends and family, but to everyone. We are custom-designed to help and be helped by others. Proverbs 11:25 NIV advises, "A generous person will prosper; whoever refreshes others will be refreshed."

Personal Insight: How have you been helped by others who were not loved ones? I challenge you to help three people in the next week.

Ninety-Seven

EMOTIONAL MIRAGE

*Y*our feelings are real, but they do not have to be your reality. Do not be deceived—your feelings are simply your *reaction* to your situation. "Whoever trusts in his own mind is a fool, but he who walks in wisdom will be delivered (Proverbs 28:26 ESV). James Allen shares, "You are today where your thoughts brought you; you will be tomorrow where your thoughts take you." If you decide everything is going wrong and the world is against you, you will disregard information that contradicts your feelings. You will become more irritable, more discouraged, more frustrated. People will avoid you more because no one wants to be around that kind of attitude. When you feel consumed by your emotions, try to draw a proverbial line between where your feelings end and your reality begins. The two do not have to be one in the same. Decide where you will draw the line.

> *Personal Insight: What reality have your thoughts created for you?*

Ninety-Eight

BE RISKY

$\mathcal{S}$uccessful people give thought to their decisions and take action. It may look crazy and risky to other people. Some may say, "You left a good paying job and took a serious pay cut, just to go chase a dream?!" Nonetheless, you can do it, if you have planned and taken potential problems into consideration. First, if your calculated risk does not work out, no worries, you will be fine. If you haven't failed at something, you must be deceased! Second, your seemingly sure thing apparently wasn't as sure as it seemed.

At any given time, the proverbial rug can be pulled from beneath us.

Recall Pastor Queen Jackson's words: "Success isn't final, and failure isn't fatal." Taking healthy risks are good for you. In the worst case scenario, it doesn't work out and you will Pick yourself up and move on.

Personal Insight: Are you willing to take risks? Why or why not?

Ninety-Nine

GIVE WITHOUT LOOKING TO RECEIVE

*H*ave you ever given a gift and then been miffed because you didn't get one back? Don't be offended. It isn't always about you. Did you give selflessly or selfishly? If you gave selfishly, then lovingly I say, "Shame on you." I have wonderful, generous friends. One good friend in particular taught me the value of this. She was out shopping one day, saw something that she knew I would like, and gave it to me. It wasn't Christmas or my birthday. It was a "just because" gift from a friend. I felt obligated to return the favor and a few weeks later, purchased a gift for her. She kindly said, "I bought you that gift because I wanted to. You do not have to buy me a gift to pay me back." It has taken me awhile to get over the knee-jerk reaction that I needed to return the favor because someone did something nice for me. Now I am comfortable giving gifts without any strings or expectations.

Paying it forward is a similar example of this strategy. A colleague registered to attend one of my workshops. She paid $89, but then found that she could not attend as she had planned. When I spoke with her about refunding her payment, she refused and asked that I apply her credit to someone who wanted to attend the workshop but could not afford it. On another occasion, I was in the grocery store with my children on Christmas Eve. A stranger stopped me and said, "Excuse me, my husband challenged me to bless someone today, and I like the way you talk to your children. You are very kind. Merry Christmas." She stuck a $50 bill in my hand and quickly walked away as I began to protest. A mix of emotions quickly brought me close to tears. Later I chuckled that she must not have been in earshot when all the children were begging for something and attempting to reach for products on the shelves. And did I mention it was Christmas Eve?!

> *Personal Insight: Are you an expectant giver or a generous one? Challenge: Pay it forward sometime in the next three days.*

One Hundred

PEOPLE ARE RESILIENT

Concern for people is good, but too often we are so afraid of whatever our imaginations have constructed that we are not proactive in doing what is in our best interest. This results in a bigger mess and increased frustration for everyone. It's easy to delude ourselves into thinking that we are protecting others, when in reality we are protecting ourselves. You will be fine, and they will be fine. No one will tie themselves to the train tracks because they are unhappy with your bombshell decision. (And if they do, it wasn't you. Trust me; they were already on their way to the tracks with rope in hand.) When we worry and do not trust others can handle it, we cripple both them and ourselves. You can take the best care of others when you do what is in their best interest, even though it may hurt their feelings.

Personal Insight: Are you putting others' needs ahead of your best interests? Why?

Appendix 1:

MORE *CHOOSE YOU!* PERSONAL INSIGHT QUESTIONS

1. What do you value most in life?
2. What are you thankful for?
3. Identify five key goals for your life.
4. Identify five people you want to nurture a relationship with.
5. Identify five new skills you want to learn in your personal life.
6. What new skills do you want to learn in your professional life?
7. What issues do you need to resolve in your personal life?

8. What issues do you need to resolve in your professional life?
9. What or who do you need to get rid of in your life?
10. What fabulous adventures do you want to indulge in?
11. Create a list of the things that make you smile.
12. What are your greatest strengths? Compare your list to the results of the free VIA Strengths Survey at http://DrElahee. pro.viasurvey.org.
13. What's your mission statement?
14. What are you going to do today to be powerful?
15. What are you going to do today to be impactful?
16. What are you going to do today to be satisfied?
17. What are you going to do today to be healthy?
18. What is your purpose?
19. What characteristics do you possess that others compliment you on and/or that you know you do well?
20. How do you use your talents and gifts?
21. What good thing do you deserve?
22. For many adults, dreams are seen as child's play. What dreams have you discarded?

23. How has fear dictated your choices and hindered you?
24. In what ways are you selling yourself short?
25. What legacy do you want to leave behind?

Appendix 2:

CHOOSE YOU! GOOD SLEEP GUIDE[1]

There is still a lot we do not know about sleep; however, we do know that getting adequate sleep is essential for good health. There are critical functions that are performed in the body during sleep. The body's hormones and metabolic processes are regulated with proper sleep. Inefficient sleep results in these vital processes operating ineffectively which in turn influences poor health and functioning.

---

1 Adapted from SleepFoundation.org

Consequences of not getting adequate sleep include: weight gain, irritability, decreased memory function, and other health problems.

» Maintain the same bedtimes and wake times even on the weekends. Keeping a set schedule will regulate your body clock and help you fall asleep.

» Have a relaxing bedtime routine that begins thirty to sixty minutes before you are ready for bed. This routine should include activities that relax and calm you and should not include activities that stress or excite you. An example of a relaxing bedtime routine may include a hot shower, soft music, and dimmed lights. This routine serves to settle down the brain and body and signals your system that you are preparing for sleep. Additionally, your evening wind-down should not include technology or television. The American Medical Association issued a policy recognizing that "exposure to excessive light at night, including extended use of various electronic media, can disrupt sleep or exacerbate sleep disorders, especially in children and adolescents." Unlike TV, these newer electronic screens are positioned close to our faces, increasing the intensity and effects of the blue light on our brains.

» Avoid naps, especially in the afternoon. However, if you absolutely need one, take a power nap. If you nap, there are two optimal choices. Set your alarm to wake after fifteen to twenty minutes of sleep *or* sleep for a full ninety minutes so that you can complete an entire sleep cycle.

» Exercise daily. The more active and vigorous your exercise, the better. Some find it best to exercise first thing in the morning, because exercising later in the day keeps them awake. Determine what works best for you.

» Make your room sleep friendly. Your bedroom should be cool—between 60 and 67 degrees. Your bedroom should be noise free. Thus, phones should be off or on silent. If your partner snores, one of you may need to sleep in a different room. Your bedroom should be dark at night, free from streetlights, yard lights, moonlight, etc. Consider using blackout curtains, eye shades, ear plugs, white-noise machines, humidifiers, fans, and other devices. Straighten your room and remove as much clutter as possible. A cluttered space is a cluttered mind, and a cluttered mind does not sleep well.

» Sleep on a comfortable mattress and pillows. The mattress you have been using for years may have exceeded its life expectancy—about nine or ten years for most good quality mattresses.

» Avoid alcohol, cigarettes, vitamins, and heavy meals in the evening, two to three hours before bedtime.

» Get a checkup. There are a number of medical concerns that can inhibit healthy sleep: arthritis, sleep apnea, chronic pain, allergies, heart disease, pregnancy, depression, and anxiety.

» Address your stress. Try deep breathing or muscle relaxation exercises to de-stress prior to sleep. If you find that every time you try to lay down, you have thoughts or concerns that keep bouncing around in your head, write them down.

Keep paper and pen by your bed. If you cannot still your thoughts, then write them down. This enables your brain to stop juggling and rest.

» Try natural over-the-counter sleep aids such as melatonin, chamomile tea, valerian root, or foods that contain tryptophan, like warm milk.

» Consult your physician.

» Try progressive muscle relaxation at bedtime. Tense up, then relax the muscles in various parts of your body until you are totally relaxed and ready to drift off.

» If you wake up during the night and can't go back to sleep, do not reward yourself by raiding the refrigerator or watching the late-late show. Such rewards will serve as an incentive to make a habit of waking up.

Thank you for purchasing this book. I pray that the book's content and your application of it will enrich your life. Send me a note via social media to let me know how *Choose You!* has impacted you.

Twitter: @LifeReignited

Facebook: www.Facebook.com/coachingforprofessionalwomen

LinkedIn: Dr. Rachel Elahee

MEET THE AUTHOR:

*D*r. Rachel Mitchum Elahee, affectionately known as Dr. Rae, is on a quest to help women live richer, more fulfilled lives. A certified diversity professional, licensed psychologist and professional coach, Dr. Rae brings a fresh approach to corporate leadership by empowering women with the practical and tangible skills necessary to achieve greater life satisfaction, professional productivity, and peace of mind.

Dr. Rae is a highly sought speaker whose audiences include conference, corporate, private interest, and civic groups. She has been featured on HLN and CBS Radio. Dr. Rae owns Elahee Psychological and works with both youth and adults. She is particularly passionate about issues faced by professional women, military veterans and their families. Additionally, Dr. Rae facilitates a group for the wives of combat veterans.

Dr. Rae is a married mother of 4 children and is active in her church and community. In addition, to spending time with family, reading is one of her favorite pastimes.

Made in the USA
Charleston, SC
27 February 2015